'I have known Cathy for many years and watched her in action as a mother, manager and leader. Her understanding of hunger and poverty, and the subsequent leadership she has taken, is based in her belief that all people are the same but conditioned differently. The resources that Cathy has mobilised around the world to end hunger are visible and impressive. As a woman leader from Africa, I'm proud to be her partner for the end of hunger. What Cathy Burke has to say should be listened to.'

Speciosa Wandira-Kazibwe
UN Secretary-General's Special Envoy for HIV/AIDS in Africa
Former Vice President of Uganda

'Cathy is a person of enormous courage, energy and devotion. She is a person of very high integrity and I hold her in enormous esteem.'

David Gonski
Chair of ANZ Bank, Chancellor, University of New South Wales

'Cathy's grasp on leadership and her ability to translate that into action is incredibly impressive. She is a brilliant communicator. She has that rare ability to connect with all people, be they CEOs, heads of state, or a poor farm worker in a village, in a way that has everyone feeling all the better for having met her.'

Michael Rennie
Global Leader, Organisation Practice, McKinsey and Co.

'The Hunger Project is winning the battle against systemic hunger by creating courageous women leaders amongst impoverished communities around the world. Cathy Burke leads THP Australia with the same courage, determination and enthusiasm.'

John Akehurst
Director, Reserve Bank of Australia

'Cathy is an inspiring and effective leader who has drawn lessons from the people whose stories she shares in this book. I've been impressed with the way she sees leadership potential in all people and seeks to help each of us be better than we ever dreamed possible.'

Diane Grady AM
Director, Macquarie Group
member of McKinsey & Co.'s Senior Advisory Board
Chair of The Hunger Project Australia

'Cathy lives and breathes a fierce commitment to women's empowerment and global issues. She is a remarkable social entrepreneur, with something profound to say about leadership and the power of humanity. At Business Chicks we showcase some of the most influential global thinkers, and Cathy is undoubtedly one of these. Through our partnership with THP, I have personally seen Cathy in action in Uganda and India, and of course Australia. She is a fresh voice of inspiration, humanity and intellect, with stories the world needs to hear.'

Emma Isaacs
CEO, Business Chicks

'Cathy Burke is such an innovative thinker and a passionate agitator for change in the world – and she does it with enormous heart, insightful vision, and an infectious sense of humour. I find her unwavering commitment to the empowerment of women and the way she engages others to inspire change incredibly positive and powerful. Her work for The Hunger Project has moved everyone at Mecca, and we're so proud to be supporting an initiative that's so committed to helping women change their present and their future.'

Jo Horgan
Mecca Cosmetica Founder and CEO

'Cathy is a fearless and courageous leader whom I admire immensely. Her perspective, based on the unusual life she has led as a leader in this global organisation, is innovative and refreshing. Cathy has the ability to have everyone feel uplifted, inspired and engaged. She has something unique and important to say, and she is able to communicate this with such lightness and grace.'

Belinda Hutchinson AM
Chancellor, University of Sydney

'Cathy Burke is one of those people that when you meet her you instantly get her passion; she is full-on about achieving big things in life ... the world needs more people like Cathy Burke.'

Richard Bowden
UK CEO, BUPA

'I remember clearly the impact Cathy first had on me at what I thought would be another routine business breakfast. I saw her understanding of women's desire to create a better future for their children and their resourcefulness to make it happen. I also saw her recognition of the importance of helping communities envision and create their own future. Cathy makes the work of The Hunger Project relevant and inspiring.'

Alison Watkins
CEO, Coca-Cola Amatil Australia

'Cathy Burke's strength lies in mobilising people and resources. She is a transformational leader who makes things happen. Cathy is one of the most inspiring women I know. She has transformed my thinking and my actions and tuned me in to a bigger game.'

Daniel Priestley
Author of *The Entrepreneur Revolution*

'Cathy is a truly unique leader. Her ability to connect with people from all walks of life is rare indeed. Cathy makes the impossible and the implausible seem remarkably achievable. Her leadership is passionate, humble and visionary. Cathy combines these attributes with genuine "out of the box" thinking.'

Symon Brewis-Weston
CEO, Sovereign Insurance

'Cathy Burke is one of life's gems. Her insights, leadership and genuine charm offensive are so contagious, one can't help but be engaged and inspired on so many levels.'

Sandra Sully
Ten Network

'Succeeding in the NGO world takes passion, patience, and persistence, as well as a well developed sense of humour. Cathy Burke has buckets of these, along with immense enthusiasm and energy for the challenge of ending world hunger. I visited a number of epicentres in Africa, one of which she had opened thirteen years earlier. The reception she received and the way she interacted with her wider 'family' was a testimony to everything she has built during her career at THP.'

Cameron O'Reilly
CEO, Bayard Capital AG

'Since I met Cathy I have been inspired by her ability to harness the strengths of those around her and create dynamic partnerships that create such a profound change. Cathy has such an open heart and brilliant mind that those around her can't help but be inspired to do more than they think they can. She is a true leader.'

Jacinta McDonell
Anytime Fitness Australia Co-Founder

Unlikely Leaders

Lessons in Leadership from the Village Classroom

Cathy Burke

Published in Australia in 2015 by Cathy Burke

Website: www.cathyburke.com

Copyright © 2015 Cathy Burke

National Library of Australia Cataloguing-in-Publication entry:
Burke, Cathy – author.

Unlikely leaders : lessons in leadership from the village classroom / by Cathy Burke.

9780994168108 (paperback)

Hunger Project
Leadership – Moral and ethical aspects
Leadership – Case studies
Conduct of life – Case studies

158.4

Cover design by Boxer & Co
Cover photo by Shehzad Noorani
Back cover photo by Millie Allbon
Printed by ExciteBooks 56487

Contents

A Note from the Author   xi

Preface   xiii

Prologue   1

1   Belief in People   5
2   Facing Reality   19
3   Vision   35
4   Personal Responsibility   51
5   Collective Power   67
6   Creating a Supportive Environment   79
7   Finding New Ways   99
8   Experiencing Success   111
9   Giving Back   121

Epilogue   133

Next Step   141

Note from the Author

I'm very excited to share this book with you, and introduce you to people who have accomplished great things, and inspired my own development as a woman and a leader. This book is both the culmination of more than twenty years' experience I've had with the global organisation, The Hunger Project and a personal reflection on what I've learned from some of the poorest people on earth.

As you read through the pages, you'll see a collection of stories and insights from truly heroic people. This book offers both a framework for creating a world of dignity and respect, and, on a personal level, lessons and perspectives on how to cope with and triumph over life's tougher challenges. With its content organised around Nine Steps of Transformative Leadership for personal and social change, it is as relevant for us in the developed world as it is for a woman farmer in Mozambique.

I regularly revisit these lessons to support my own journey in life. Whenever I'm dealing with personal or professional challenges, these stories and the framework of thinking represented help me repower my own life. I apply these Nine Steps of Transformative Leadership with wonderful results. The people you'll meet in this book remind me that I am more than my circumstances and the stuff that happens to me. We can each demonstrate agency, influence and empowerment that need not be limited by what is happening around us. I encourage you to dive into this book with a fearless and open heart.

I hope that in reading this book you too will be deeply inspired by the leadership concepts outlined and the people who live them. While some of the stories are confronting and challenging, many are completely heart lifting. They all have one common thread – the innate power of the human spirit. It is my belief that every single one of us can create extraordinary change in our own lives and communities. We can all demonstrate leadership – and this is needed now more than ever before. Even in the most poverty stricken places where opportunities are seemingly next to nil, people are assuming responsibility and achieving incredible things. They are the torchbearers for a new humanity.

Cathy Burke

Preface

Over the last twenty years with The Hunger Project, it has been my privilege to travel extensively across the villages of Africa and South Asia. As the Chief Executive Officer of The Hunger Project Australia, I've been exposed to some of the most unexpected and confronting experiences of my life. I've sat with people on dirt floors, under trees and in small tin sheds, learning about their lives and challenges. I've held babies who I knew would die and I've conversed with women through the thin bamboo walls of their hut, outside which they are not permitted to show their faces.

These experiences have shaped me profoundly as a human being and a leader. In reflecting on my time spent with people from various villages in Africa and South Asia, key themes emerged, and contrary to what you might expect, they were not themes of desperation and misery. Rather, they were strong messages of courage, boldness and vision. What I've seen and what the people I've met have given me are the most enduring lessons in life and leadership. These women and men are truly the *Unlikely Leaders*. They are at the forefront of demonstrating what it takes to evolve, lead and grow in the harshest of conditions. Empowered, they can, will and do come up with innovative, practical and long-lasting solutions to the issues they face. They are the ones who will end the global problem of hunger once and for all.

With a specific focus on personal leadership and transformation, these enduring lessons have become the foundation of this book. When reading through the book, you'll notice each of the stories is grouped under nine chapters. This framework structure represents the Nine Steps of Transformative Leadership I have observed personally. By presenting the material in this way, I offer you what I believe is a surprising journey towards leadership. Every chapter covers key concepts which build upon one another. Commencing with the founding principle that people can achieve more than their current condition seemingly permits, the book goes on to explore leadership distinctions including the potency of the right mindset, the power of the collective, and giving back. Each of the Nine Steps of Transformative Leadership contains a collection of personal stories from village people across Africa and South Asia which are designed to illustrate specific leadership traits such as resilience, courage, bravery and boldness.

At the end of each story, I've included a 'Things to Think About' break-out box. The stories and people in this book offer new perspectives, and these reflections in the break-out boxes are designed to give you some space to think about how this applies to you. I encourage you to dig in and reflect back on your own life in these sections. The only exception to this is Chapter 2, which is designed to be a stand-alone section.

Some of the personal case studies and stories described in this book are not easy. Many of them show the different faces of chronic persistent hunger. I have included them to help you understand the heroic journey undertaken by the people featured. By understanding something of their background, their accomplishments are all the more humbling and remarkable. These stories are all true, but for privacy reasons, I've changed some of the names of people in this book.

My intention is for this book to demonstrate and illuminate the inner personal leaps we are all capable of making in order to harness the full power of human potential. In sharing these stories about courageous leaders, my hope is to inspire your own leadership promise. For humanity to be equal to the task of our many challenges – including ending hunger – we all need to move out of our smallness. Only then can we own and act on the power we have to shape the world we want to live in.

The book's focus on the personal is not intended in any way to negate the need to strive for social change. This book isn't supposed to be a 'pick yourself up by your bootstraps' exhortation. Profound change also needs to take place in the way that our world and societies are organised. Many of the gains we currently enjoy were hard won by people who challenged and transformed the previous status quo.

I believe every single person is equipped with the fundamental and innate power for extraordinary transformative change. Like the people in this book, I've personally lived it, and maybe you have too. Furthermore, I believe the capacity we all have for leadership is often not expressed or acknowledged. For all our education and wealth, many of us still have an attitude of 'Who, me?' and deny the power we each have to take action. Many of us are *Unlikely Leaders* in hiding.

I share these stories and insights without any intent to diminish the often inspiring qualities of leadership we see in developed parts of the world. The lessons I've learned in developing villages cut through differences in circumstances to something deeper we can all relate to. As the great mythologist and thinker Joseph Campbell observed: 'Every life has heroic potential.' Through my work in the field of combatting world hunger, I've witnessed the fulfilment of that heroic potential countless times. These experiences have given me a unique perspective on leadership. Most importantly, they ignite a brilliant torch for all of us regarding what it means to be human.

Personally, I am passionate about creating a shift in our thinking and ability to make a difference. More than twenty years ago, my passion led me to The Hunger Project; a global organisation committed to ending hunger. I love this work because it focuses on the *human component* of ending world hunger. The Hunger Project stems from a profound belief that people are extraordinary. Human beings everywhere have enormous capacities for profound trans-formations, insights, renewal and change. The Hunger Project has fostered this understanding and pioneered sustainable and effective on-the-ground strategies in twelve countries, which, in turn, has had an impact on more than twenty million people. More than four hundred thousand local volunteers have been trained to take action to end hunger in their communities. The Hunger Project creates and builds leaders.

The women and men in this book show us the way forward. They are achieving outcomes for their communities that are totally unexpected. Their actions are lessons in courage, boldness and resil-ience. They are feeding their children, getting water to their village, raising their voices to be heard, and exercising their legal and moral rights. They are true leaders in every sense of the word.

Prologue

Ethiopia, 1992.

About eight of us – all investors in The Hunger Project – piled into rattling four-wheel drive vehicles and headed off to the villages. We were in Ethiopia as part of the Africa Prize for Leadership for the Sustainable End of Hunger, and our visit included meeting rural farmers and families miles away from the capital, Addis Ababa.

On the way to our destination we had to drive through a place, which, at that time, was referred to as the 'Valley of Death'. It was so named because less than ten years earlier during the famine of the mid-eighties, one hundred thousand people (mainly women and children) had died while on the move searching for food and water. Driving through this valley was sobering and deeply moving.

After many hours, we arrived at a cluster of mud huts called Goda-Chili. This is not a place you will find on any map. It barely resembled a village, let alone a town. When I stepped out of the vehicle, I was unaware I was about to participate in one of the most defining experiences of my life.

Being in Goda-Chili was to be my first real interaction with people living with hunger. At this time, I was a young mum in my twenties from my own small world in Australia. I wasn't an aid worker, nor was I experienced in 'off the beaten track' travel. Nothing could have prepared me for what I saw and felt that day as I stepped out of the jeep and looked around. I felt very nervous and acutely disconnected, like I was an alien who had been beamed

1

down from another planet. It felt like I was in an alternate reality. Was this the same Earth?

Greeting us were mothers with droopy, empty breasts and babies suckling for no reward. Some of the women wore no shirts, and their faces were exceptionally hard. What I witnessed was chronic, persistent hunger, pushed yet again towards famine by drought. The parched, sun-crazed earth stretched featureless in all directions. The villagers' meagre maize crop that should have stood tall at this time of the year was inches high and pitifully sparse – far off yielding anything edible. People were ground down by day-in, day-out malnutrition.

I walked around their huts feeling distressed. They were classic round mud huts with straw on top; however, as if affected by the same malaise as the crop surrounding them, they were diminished and dilapidated. Many huts had holes in the walls and the straw looked like ageing wisps of hair. I nearly tripped over a man who was lying on the ground. He did not move. I found out later that he was willing himself to die so he would not be a burden on his community any longer.

It was very upsetting. I questioned what I was doing there. I can't describe how awkward I felt. I felt like I didn't belong, and wondered what we could possibly have in common with this community.

I watched in awe as the leader of our group greeted the local people. Her name was Lynne Twist, and she was a long-term leader in The Hunger Project. She was warm and connected. She spoke to people through an interpreter. Sometimes she would disappear into the huts to speak privately to the women.

I was so confronted. What I was seeing was not some horrific sideshow. It was not an aberration. The most disturbing part was the emerging awareness that this is how a billion people – a billion brothers and sisters with whom we share our planet – live their daily lives.

The villagers crowded around, and the tribal chief welcomed us. He was a tall and commanding man. Lynne spoke on behalf of our group and shared that we were from The Hunger Project and were deeply committed to ending hunger. She further explained that we were not offering food or aid. Instead she said, 'We have come to hear from you, to learn your stories, to understand what you are up against and to take your message out into the world to end hunger. We will tell your story and make you visible.'

I was listening to this, desperately trying not to cry. The people of Goda-Chili were standing with great dignity, and the last thing I wanted to do was blubber all over the place. Inwardly, I was casting harsh judgements on Lynne's words, thinking how inadequate it all sounded.

And then the chief spoke. He welcomed us, stating that no one had visited his village in more than twenty years. He told us his community did not want anything from us. They were experiencing hard times, but they would survive. His next words blew my heart open: 'As a result of this meeting, if our people's life and death means that others do not have to live and die like us, our lives will then be worth something.'

I could scarcely contain what he said, and the dignity and pride of his community. His courage and insight was humbling beyond words.

We travelled back to our little shack where we were staying and pandemonium broke out. Everyone was devastated. We'd spent time with people who had nothing, and we'd done nothing about it. We just talked to them. People were upset and angry. 'We had biscuits and blankets, and we gave nothing!' cried one of the people on the trip. And then the conversation took place that was to change the direction of my life.

Lynne reminded us that they had not asked for anything and they were clear about that. 'You want to give purely for your own selfish reasons,' she said. 'You want to make yourself feel better; to assuage some of the horror you saw today. Giving blankets or biscuits would only let you off the hook and trick you into thinking you made a difference, when you have not.' And then the kicker: 'The only thing to do is keep your promise to these people. Be their voice and go out into the world and do what's needed to end hunger.'

I felt like I had been knighted with a sacred task. This book is an extension of my promise that day to the women and men I met in Goda-Chili – part of my commitment to make them visible. Hundreds of millions of people worldwide wake up to unimaginable hardship, and each day they manage to feed themselves and their families as best they can. They do this unacknowledged and invisible. They are often perceived as a problem when, in fact, they are incredibly innovative, hard-working and resourceful. They are the solution and their empowerment is the key to combatting hunger and poverty.

Belief in People

The first step in the Nine Steps of Transformative Leadership is to recognise our own innate ability. The unerring truth at the heart of this book is that only you can author your own life. You are an agent for change. You are capable of transformation. And so is everyone else.

We all have the potential for leadership but sometimes we think we don't or others don't. It's confronting to think of ourselves in this way. We argue for our limitations, or for the shortcomings of people we perceive as being less smart than us. We look up to people who have accomplished things we admire and, comparing ourselves, we think we can never achieve anything remotely similar. We diminish ourselves before we even start. I've seen this the world over. We think we are defined by our circumstances, or that our past determines our future. We believe that people are victims and it's not possible to respond in any other way. We can feel helpless – about ourselves or others. It's very human and it's also not true.

This lack of honouring our power and capacity stands in the way of us being able to create and realise a better future. This is true whether you live in Sydney or Ouagadougou. Sustainable change can only happen when we truly understand that we are sufficient. We have what it takes! There is no saviour or outside force coming to rescue us. It is up to us to solve our problems – personally and collectively – and we are up to the challenge!

In this context, where each and every person can be part of the solution, we all contribute something valuable. There are no unequal players. We each have something to offer. This change in perspective from hopeless victim to taking full ownership – a 'this is my life and my village and I'm going to take action' mentality is crucial to fostering sustainable change. It's available to all of us. It's part of our birthright as human beings.

Consistent with this concept is a common myth that we are all separate. We live like we're not connected, and that what happens in one place does not have an impact anywhere else. It takes a certain generosity of spirit to break through this notion of separateness; an inclusiveness to see that there is actually no difference between me 'over here' and a villager 'over there'. We are all capable of intelligence, creativity, and courage. We all share the same desires, hopes and dreams.

The deeper truth about who we really are as people is that, not only does our existence affect each and every other person, but ultimately we *are* one another. If someone is capable of stepping up to assume a leadership role, then we all are. A woman farmer in India, when reflecting upon the ripple effect of seeing other non-literate women farmers lead in her community told me, 'If she can do it, so can I!' And she's right! Each choice we make and every action we take is inextricable from the global whole. What we do and what we don't do has an impact on our world.

Having an absolute belief and faith in people's innate ability to decide themselves on the direction of their own lives is the crucial first step. Believe in people! That fact that this concept is so little understood gives it the potency to make a huge difference in the lives of many individuals and communities.

In this chapter you'll meet people who are living examples of this reality. Flora from Malawi shares her experience of growing into an admired contributor to her community despite her initial lack of belief that this was possible. Living in a small village in Bangladesh, Keya was a young woman who demonstrates how her difficult life became the inspiration to make a difference in other people's lives.

The people in this chapter illustrate how human capacity for profound transformation and leadership can arise anywhere. Nothing can be achieved until we own our individual capacity for growth.

FLORA – SHOWING UP CHANGES LIVES

In landlocked, famine-prone Malawi, I became friends with a woman called Flora. She had become an influential leader in her small country village, and her story of growth is remarkable.

About seven years before we first met, Flora lived in a thatched one-room hut with dirt walls. During the rainy season, her hut leaked. She tended a small garden but was only able to grow enough for subsistence. She and her husband Peter were farmers and had uncertain food security. All the other people in their surrounding village were in a similar situation.

A team from The Hunger Project Malawi came to her village to talk about ending hunger and see whether the community could be mobilised. Like the other villagers, Flora felt quite cynical about the notion of ending hunger in her poor village. She laughed as she reminisced to me how strange it sounded at the time that hunger could be ended; particularly as there were no food trucks or money vans accompanying these claims. Even more surprising for her was how The Hunger Project particularly sought out women with whom to have this discussion. Women were more than just tolerated; they were asked to sit up the front at meetings and share their thoughts and opinions. This was a completely new concept.

At the first meeting, people gathered to hear two incredible things. Firstly, the idea that hunger could end. Secondly, that it would be the villagers themselves who would play the lead role in creating change. These concepts were unbelievable for Flora. The very thought that hunger could end was fanciful. It was not as though they had thought about it and dismissed the idea – such an idea had never even been conceived. Behind her incredulity, however, Flora said she felt something stirring within her, but it was too nascent to be articulated.

After that first meeting, the people of the village all returned to their homes. They lit fires and prepared dinner. People met and spoke amongst themselves about what they had just heard. Flora said the people were extremely cynical at first – the thought of playing a role in forging a better life for themselves was so foreign. Was it a trick? How could this be possible? There was no way it could work. It just did not make sense. It seemed like a better idea not to risk anything and carry on as usual. Besides, everyone was too busy just trying to survive.

The high level of scepticism from the first conversation could have ended the whole project. However, a certain number of the villagers – including Flora and her husband Peter – returned the next day to hear more. Even though the concept seemed unattainable, there was something about it that enticed them to go back 'for another look'. The conversation continued. What followed is a humbling reminder that one key element for transformation is just 'showing up'.

I met Flora seven years after this benchmark conversation. By this stage, she was a successful pig farmer, and her community was thriving. She now lived in a four-room brick home with an iron roof. Using money she had borrowed from The Hunger Project microfinance scheme, she had started out with one piglet. Microfinance involves lending small amounts of money (mainly to women) for income generating opportunities. The average first loan is usually about $50 and training is a requirement to being permitted to borrow.

Flora cared for the piglet, which eventually attracted a good market price, enabling her to buy more piglets. She learned how to grow more produce in her garden and how to make secondary food products from her crops. Flora was teaching jam making to other women in the village and other ways of preserving food, so it would last during the leaner months. She paid for the education of a number of orphan children. Her life had completely turned around from the initial moment The Hunger Project arrived.

It is easy to match a successful person against their achievements when they have already achieved success. However, it's harder to see where they came from and what unseen personal transformations took place before change occurred. Speaking to Flora about her development was fascinating and made me reflect on my own circumstances. It is sometimes easier to be suspicious or cynical; easier to hang on to all our old reasons and stories about why we should not engage. We tend to hedge our bets, trying to figure out beforehand if something is going to be worth our while. Flora taught me the power of showing up; participating in the conversation and seeing it through to the end. Failure to show up is a crucial part of why we do not achieve what we are capable of.

Things to think about: SHOWING UP

∿ How many times have you been asked, but declined, to attend something that might challenge your thinking; that might inspire you or bring you joy? It could be a singing class ('Me, sing?'), or a networking event that could be beneficial for your business but you won't know anyone. ('Too scary!'). Flora highlights what's available when we push through those fears and show up!

∿ In the face of scepticism, the ability to 'take a second look' can be the catalyst for transformation. Even better is the resolve to keep turning up – and witness the change unfold!

∿ Your community wants you to show up. Resist the urge to play it safe. Observe the changes Flora made which had a direct impact on others. By changing her life she was able to nurture, teach and empower others, leaving a legacy that was larger than her.

KEYA – BECOMING A ROLE MODEL

I visited a small village in Bangladesh, not far from Khulna. There, I met a young woman called Keya. At this stage, Keya was eighteen years old. She had been married at the age of twelve and gave birth to her first child when she was fourteen.

Child marriage is all too common in Bangladesh. One in three girls is married by the time they reach fifteen years of age. Of these, sixty per cent are pregnant within the first year. A staggering seventy-four per cent of Bangladeshi girls are married before the legal age of eighteen. Early marriage entrenches a cycle of poverty and powerlessness in these girl's lives. It reinforces the problem of malnutrition because young and undernourished girls give birth to low-birth-weight babies. In addition, young girls' bodies have not yet matured, so they are at risk of increased birthing complications, including obstructed labour, fistula and death.

According to UNICEF's 2011 State of the World's Children report, girls who become pregnant before the age of sixteen are three to four times more likely to die while giving birth than women in their twenties.

Keya was lucky because she survived the birth of her child. However, she lacked opportunity and education. Because she was married, her freedom of movement was curtailed, as was her ability to complete her schooling.

In Keya's village, The Hunger Project had already trained a number of women volunteer leaders called 'Unleashed Women Leaders'. These local women lived in the village and experienced the same difficulties that other women faced. However, as trained leaders, they were now able to bravely confront the status quo. These Unleashed Women Leaders were uncompromising, focused and inclusive. They would go from hut to hut, talking to women like Keya, and bringing them together to discuss issues and help take the necessary action to lift themselves out of poverty.

One focus of the Unleashed Women Leaders was to dispel myths around women's health, such as one concerning pregnancy. In parts of rural Bangladesh, people believe that eating less when pregnant will aid childbirth. Unfortunately, this only leads to the development of a malnourished baby and a weakened mother. Consequently, the Unleashed Women Leaders made it their mission to educate women about feeding and nourishing themselves as a priority for both their own and their baby's wellbeing.

Looking out from the confines of her hut, Keya noticed these women leaders. To her, they seemed to be full of purpose. They were creating positive change in her village and taking action to help the community grow. They were not in it for themselves, and their actions benefitted everyone in one way or another. A community with healthy women and babies results in a healthy community for everyone.

Keya felt a burning desire to be like them. In fact, she wanted to be one of these Unleashed Women Leaders. While talking to her, I could just imagine this young girl gazing out unobserved at the work these courageous women were doing.

Keya spoke to one of these women about her desire to become an Unleashed Woman Leader and was soon trained by The Hunger Project. She did the four-day residential leader training and committed herself to effect positive changes within her village. After her training, young Keya became a role model for others.

One of the first things Keya did was set up a women's self-help group in her village. She went door to door inviting other women to join her group. This was not an easy mission. However, because other women leaders had run successful self-help groups with a positive outcome, the village women were willing to trust her and give it a go. She ended up recruiting twenty-six members who met on a weekly basis to support each other in taking action to lift their status.

Keya motivated and supported the women in this group. I attended one of their meetings and met the women involved. Most were non-literate, and many had been married very young. Their ages ranged from eighteen to some much older ladies who did not know how old they were. All lived in very poor circumstances and were malnourished; however, each member made a commitment to bring along ten to fifteen taka (about eleven cents) each week to pool as a kitty for entrepreneurial endeavours. This act alone was an enormous commitment toward the women's own self-reliance.

Keya embodied the behaviour she encouraged within the self-help group. She too saved money. She urged all of the women to keep attending the meetings. Within eighteen months, these women had not only pooled savings from subscriptions, but had created their own microfinance facility by investing the money back into the group. The investments were repaid with interest and had grown to a pool of fifty-two thousand taka (AUD$800), with a further seventy-two thousand taka (AUD$1,000) loaned out at that time.

Members used this seed capital to establish small businesses. I spoke to some of the women and heard about how they were doing extraordinary things. A number of them had set up small poultry businesses, raising chickens and selling eggs. Some had started sewing businesses, while others made cardboard boxes for local stores to sell their wares in. These micro-enterprises, born from the resourcefulness of these women under Keya's leadership, were truly inspiring.

Keya confided in me that she has resolved to establish a major campaign within her village to stamp out child marriages within two years. She is passionate about making sure no other young girl should suffer as she did, so she is mobilising the village to make child marriage a thing of the past. She is fully supported by the other volunteer women leaders. I have no doubt she will achieve her goal.

Keya is now a role model for many of the women in her village. Yet Keya became the person she is today as a result of the example set by the Unleashed Women Leaders in her village. These women did not know Keya was observing them from the sidelines. They were not playing to their perceived audience. Instead, they were acting in alignment with their vision and the values they espoused by becoming firm advocates and activists for other women and girls. Role modelling was effective in creating other leaders precisely because it was authentic and had actions matching intentions. Because of Keya's leadership, together with the other Unleashed Women Leaders, there is now a strongly embedded image within her village of purposeful and empowered women who stand up for what is right.

I sometimes think of young Keya standing in the doorway of her hut, looking out into the village. She was unnoticed, but she saw the other women leaders' activities and felt their presence. How long was she watching them for? How long did she observe their actions? How many times did she see intention matching action through the work of the women leaders? All of this served to deeply nourish and nurture within her a heartfelt desire to become a leader herself.

Things to think about: BEING A ROLE MODEL

- ❖ Keya's story demonstrates that we are all role models. Whether you're aware of it or not, your behaviour is being observed by others. Keya reminds us that we are always a role model for someone. Be aware of what's happening around you because ultimately your actions have the power to influence others.

- ❖ After being influenced by others, Keya herself became a role model. Surely this is one of the greatest outcomes of being a leader – namely, building other leaders through your own actions. Who is observing you and what you do from the sidelines? Who are you influencing unintentionally?

- Who are your role models? When carefully selected, role models can help provide you with a blueprint for leadership.

DIFFERENT: SAME

How do you start the process of shifting entrenched debilitating beliefs, or the disabling mindset of a community? The best way involves tapping into people's own desire for change. Antoine de Saint-Exupéry captured this beautifully in this quote: 'If you want to build a ship, don't drum up the men to gather wood, divide the work and give orders. Instead, teach them to yearn for the vast and endless sea.'

This process of shifting beliefs can only start with people recognising their capabilities. None of us have a fatal flaw that pre-disposes all our efforts to be doomed.

Let me give you an example from Malawi of how this principle plays out in action through the Vision, Commitment and Action Workshop (VCA). In these workshops – which may consist of only a few people or may have hundreds in attendance – people consider what their village could look like when free from hunger. The Hunger Project designed the Vision, Commitment and Action Workshop as an antidote to resignation and as a way to directly enable people to be agents of their own life. Each workshop is led by trained volunteer leaders called *animators* who come from within the community itself. The main focuses for the workshops are: creating a vision for your life; committing to it; and taking personal and collective action.

During this particular Vision, Commitment and Action workshop, the animator was helping rural farmers to recognise that they are capable, intelligent beings. He did this by comparing the villagers to people from overseas.

The first step involves the Malawian animator tacking up a piece of butcher's paper to the trunk of a tree. In front of him are about seventy farmers. Women sit in the front and men sit at the back of the group. Most have come directly from the fields. They work hard and other than a few crops they sell for cash, they eat what they grow. If they cannot grow sufficient crops, then they do not eat.

For three to four months when the harvest food supplies are at their lowest ebb, many families are not able to meet their nutritional and calorie needs.

The animator asks the assembly an interesting question: 'What do American farmers look like?' He elaborates: 'They can feed themselves. They have food to send to us. How come they can grow so much? They have so much left over. Are they superhuman? Do they have two sets of arms?' He asks them to list what an American farmer looks like and begins to draw a picture from the description people give him. People call out what they think they look like, and the answers flow: two arms, two legs, one pair of eyes, one head, ten fingers.

The trainer moves to a tree nearby. The community turns around to see him standing next to another tree with butcher's paper tacked on it. 'What do we look like in Malawi?' People call out, 'Two arms, two legs, one pair of eyes, one head, ten fingers.'
Then the trainer takes the two pieces of paper and puts them together. Voila! People see that there is nothing missing or different in the physical make up or capacity of the farmers in the two drawings. This is a revelation! While we might read this and think, 'Of course!' for many of these villagers this is a real 'Aha!' moment. This sinks in even deeper when the trainer asks them to point out the differences, and of course there are none. We are all human. He then teases out the realisation that there is no special ability or power an American farmer has that Malawians do not have. We all work. We all have the same physical attributes.

The question of race does come up. 'But we are black!' is proposed by some of the villagers as a reason why they cannot grow enough food. The animator cuts through this objection: 'Our skin might be black, but they have black skinned farmers too! What colour is the American farmers' blood?' He speaks of this difference as being literally skin deep. If we were to peel back that thinnest layer of difference, we are still all the same underneath. Skin colour has no bearing on ability and does not confer superhuman innate qualities. This makes sense and the people agree.

These workshops are the first part of a long process to shift people's mindsets. They start to break down entrenched myths that local people can't do anything to change their situation, and the power to feed them resides in people living far away, through food drops and the like. Now this may sound simplistic and not particularly sophisticated, but at heart we humans are pretty simple. Faced with adversity and loss of direction, we might believe, 'we are a special case', which, in turn, can cause inaction. We are not. This vivid process is effective in reframing how people see themselves and their capacities, and serves to kindle an awareness of what might be possible.

Things to think about: SIMILARITIES & DIFFERENCES

❧ When you think you are different from someone else and use that as an excuse for not trying, think again. We are more similar than we think. Our capacity to create, imagine and dare is not a characteristic of one person and denied to someone else. Nor does it belong to one country, gender or race, and not another. We are each capable of accomplishing something that leaves our world all the richer for us having been in it.

❧ Give up thinking you aren't any good. Look for similarities. Learn from people who have done it before you, and take heart that if they can do it, so can you!

❧ When you hear that others have achieved something enormously powerful, use it to inspire you and give you the confidence to dream big and take the action to make it happen.

Facing Reality

Facing up to reality, or 'confronting what's so' is the powerful second step in the Nine Steps of Transformative Leadership. Unfortunately, this step is often skipped over because it's just too uncomfortable.

As a society, we find many ways to avoid opening our eyes to what's really happening. We look away because we don't want to feel bad. This isn't surprising. The way in which problems in the world are discussed often reinforces powerlessness. It can all seem so hopeless. We do this in our personal lives as well. Instead of seeing things as they really are, we create excuses which, in turn, can keep us trapped in denial and futility.

People sometimes think that facing up to reality leads to negativity and a dark chasm. 'Oh, the world's so terrible with all this awful stuff going on. What can I do? It's so depressing.' Paradoxically, submitting to the idea that things will never change causes more suffering. This is because it forces us to function on top of an internalised sense of despair. We can easily prove ourselves right by never

19

doing anything about it. Interestingly, when we can observe and bear witness to how things are *right now* – without judgment and blame – the right and appropriate action becomes available and apparent. Something arises within us once we have courage to assess and own our current reality. It's only when we recognise where we're at, that we can know where to go to from there.

It is liberating to face your situation; to look at an issue without any subtext of blame and make a commitment to resolve it. It's a powerful and profound tool in creating change. It may seem a bit Zen, but it's true: the degree to which you can authentically be with something without shrinking from it, is the degree to which you can transform it.

The stories in this chapter are not easy. Stories such as Mohan's heartbreaking choice between feeding his family and taking his sick son to receive medical treatment, and Adia's struggle to comfort her hungry children show the different faces of chronic persistent hunger. I've included them because hunger is the biggest human rights issue facing us on earth. It cuts across so many of the issues that confront us as human beings. Hunger is the unspoken background to many of the stories in this book.

This is the only chapter that does not include the 'Things to Think About' break-out box after each story. As you read this chapter, keep your mind and heart open. In doing so, a new course of action or engagement might occur to you.

INVISIBLE HUNGER

Uganda is such a beautiful country. It is very similar landscape to where I live in eastern Australia. The sub-tropical landscape is lush and verdant with rich red volcanic soils.

A few years ago, I visited an area near Mbale called Iganga. These villages were some kilometres off the major road. Even though Mbale was a small bustling town, to the people of Iganga it seemed as though it was light years away. The roads were dirt tracks, so for some months of the year, when the rain was exceedingly heavy, even four-wheel drive vehicles couldn't get through. It was quite inaccessible. The Hunger Project was aiming to work in Iganga, and I was travelling with our local staff to meet the people and hear about their issues.

Arriving in the area, it was easy to mistakenly think I was in paradise. The children were beautiful, and the women were warm and welcoming. I sat with a group of women. Some were preparing maize for dinner by separating the dried kernels from the cob and pounding them into flour. Others were weaving mats out of straw. Babies were at the breast or lying on mats beside their mums or their aunties. In the fading afternoon light, it appeared to be a serene and beautiful scene.

However, almost every woman I spoke with lived solely on a diet of cassava and sweet potato. Occasionally they had a bit of maize. That was it. No protein. No other vegetables. The women were able to feed their families two meals a day of this monotonous and inadequately nutritious fare. A number of women could only manage to feed their children once a day. One mother explained to me that she had to carefully time the daily meal. If she fed her children too early, they wouldn't be able to sleep because of the hunger. If she fed them too late, they would be too hungry and listless to do anything during the day. This is the reality of chronic hunger.

A few kilometres down the track from this community, there were a number of villagers for whom one meal a day was the limit they could produce. A young boy had broken his arm two weeks earlier, and it had not been set. He had been climbing a tree looking for fruit and he fell. His arm was misshapen and angular. Even though a medical clinic was located only about ten kilometres away, his mother wasn't able to take him. She had seven other children to watch over and to try and feed. Her children were listless, and their shaven heads scarred with ringworm.

This apparent paradise lost its shine for me that day. Chronic hunger is so pernicious, persistent and hidden. You can't see it sometimes unless you look beyond what is immediately obvious. Even when food is grown, nearly half can spoil through insecure storage practices. Mould, rodents and insects can decimate food stores. Imagine how heartbreaking this is. This isn't famine. It is chronic, persistent hunger. This is the reality for the 840 million people who live with it on an ongoing daily basis.

That day I felt so relieved for this community – at least there was hope that their future would be different. The Hunger Project was commencing its work there. Women would be educated. Food would be stored safely. A community would be mobilised. Health care would be within walking distance. Nevertheless, in Africa, a lot more work needs to be done in order to create a better future.

MOHAN – BREAKING STONES

How can we live in a world with so much sorrow? We have to allow it in to shape us, and not drown or numb us.

The state of Madhya Pradesh is a poor region, part of the so-called 'Hindi Belt' across north eastern India. In an area about three hundred kilometres from the capital of Bhopal, I met Mohan, his wife and their young son. They lived in a one-room hut, barely two by three-and-a-half metres, amidst a hot, dry and rocky landscape. A plastic mat on the floor served as the bed they all shared. There were a couple of pots and some old clothes folded neatly in the corner. A thatched roof meant that when it rained the family got wet.

Mohan stood very tall, and I was immediately struck by his pride and love for his family. He worked as a bonded labourer in a stony field about three kilometres away from his home. His work involved breaking the stones in the field in preparation for planting. He earned fifty rupees a day (about US $1) doing this mindless backbreaking work. He was considered lucky because, as a bonded labourer, he had secure work all year round. The trade-off for this stability was less pay per day than a daily wage labourer. There were no benefits or allowances. If he did not work, he didn't get paid. This practice is actually illegal in India. But like many laws, it is often not enforced.

It is unusual in these remote parts of India to find a family with only one child. While visiting Mohan and his small family, he shared his story with me. A few years prior, the family had an older child who became ill. The mother tended to him the best she could while her husband walked to the fields and worked every day, breaking stones. It became apparent that the child needed medical attention. The nearest hospital was a full day's travel, requiring a five-hour walk to the main road followed by a four-hour bus ride. The mother was not strong enough to carry her sick son that distance, especially with a toddler in tow. They would also need to stay for a few days as it could take that long for the sick child to receive medical treatment.

It meant that Mohan would have to take the child. After an agonising deliberation, they decided that the family could not afford the father to spend time away from working the field, as any absence meant a loss of wages for that period. If Mohan were to take his son to the hospital, attend to him for a number of days and then return home, it would seriously jeopardise their already precarious financial situation. As it was, they were barely living day-to-day. The wellbeing of the entire family was at stake.

Mohan had to keep working in order to sustain his family, while his wife tried to keep their son as comfortable as possible and pray for a miracle. Each day for a week, Mohan would get up and walk the three kilometres to the field. He spent the day breaking stones on a landlord's field, knowing his son was at home dying. Sadly, a miracle didn't come soon enough for their son.

This encounter shook me to my core. I simply could not imagine being in a situation where I was forced to make that sort of decision. They had to choose between life for their son and life for the family. I regularly think of Mohan and his family. It helps to keep me strong and focused. World hunger just has to end. It is so demeaning and so cruel.

ADIA – STONE STEW

I travelled to Ethiopia less than ten years after the big famine of the mid-eighties. Visiting some nearby villages, I wandered off down a dirt track where I met Adia. She lived with her family of six children under a dwelling of leaves, sticks and old bags. There was no husband.

I sat on the ground to talk to Adia and heard about her mental anguish. She told me there was not enough food to feed her children. Her explanation of how she coped with this situation on the days where there wasn't enough food for her family broke my heart. On days when food was scarce, Adia would put some stones in a pot as if she was cooking them. If she had enough fuel, she would light a small fire of twigs and place the pot full of stones on top.

Her children would be crying from hunger. They would ask her what they could eat. And she would point to the pot and say, 'It's nearly ready. The meal is nearly ready to eat. It won't be long now.' The children were momentarily appeased, hopeful that food was on its way. Eventually, they would fall asleep before the 'meal' was cooked, and so another day went by.

I can hardly imagine being this mother. Not having enough food to feed my children, and having to find ways to distract them from their hunger pains. It's just not right.

CYCLE OF MALNUTRITION

Many things occur in cycles: seasons, fashion and political parties. But some cycles seem to continue indefinitely. They run a longer span and they can remain unnoticed.

The cycle of malnutrition is one such thing. It can span a lifetime and, in many areas, it has lasted for generations. It is a cycle that involves severe disempowerment of women and girls, and its effects are widespread.

The Cycle of Malnutrition starts at birth. Girls are born into families that all too often wanted and prayed for a son.

There are many towns and villages across South Asia where the sex ratio is heavily distorted in favour of males: it is not uncommon in some areas for there to be only seven hundred females for every one thousand males. This is not accidental.

One of the driving reasons for these missing girl babies is the belief that boys are better for a family, and girls are a liability. With a girl, you are expected to spend money on a dowry. A boy can perform the religious rites when parents die. When a daughter marries, she leaves you for another family and you may never see her again. A son remains with you forever; often living in the same compound, raising his family in your village. There is a 'blessing' uttered to a bride when she is married: 'May you be the mother of a hundred sons.'

When boys are born, there is great celebration. Drums are banged and sweets are given. When a girl is born there is nothing. Silence. I have met women who are the second- or third-born girl in their families, and their name, in the local language, means 'enough'.

Nowadays, across India, the dearth of baby girls is aided by sex selection abortion through ultrasound clinics. Tucked away in some of the most remote corners of the country where access to even the most basic healthcare is scarce, these clinics are not designed to protect the health and wellbeing of the mother or child. They are available for families to find out whether they are having a boy or a girl, and if the latter, they are given the option to terminate the pregnancy. In the past, you would see billboards in Hindi and other languages across the country advertising: 'Spend 5,000 rupees now and save 500,000 later.' (Thankfully this practice has now been outlawed).

Before sex-selected abortions became so commonplace, infanticide of newborn daughters pushed this tragedy beyond clinical. When an unwanted girl was born, the midwife would hold the baby down while the mother or the mother-in-law poured rock salt down the baby's throat to kill her. Sometimes the baby was smothered. For this action, the midwife was paid a few extra rupees. Other times, the baby was just not fed and left to starve.

The next stage of the Cycle of Malnutrition starts with feeding. When a girl is born, she is weaned faster in the hope that the mother will soon fall pregnant again – this time with a boy. Breastfeeding provides essential nutrients and prevents the infant from drinking contaminated water. When a girl comes off the breast, she is often fed a mixture of water sweetened with sugar.

There is an insightful video by UNICEF, which shows a set of twins raised by their mother. The babies were born a similar birth weight, but months later the boy is thriving, whereas the baby girl is emaciated. The parents will say it's because she has a 'throat infection', which the visiting doctor can find no evidence of. The girl is starving because anything extra – including her share – goes to her brother. Often, a new mother comes from a family that is so poor that she must go back to work in the fields right after birth, and has no time to breastfeed. Her daughter is just fed rice gruel or unclean water sweetened with sugar. This lack of care for a daughter is entrenched and deadly.

The next stage of the cycle is lack of education. The girl attends to the chores at an early age and is often kept out of school to help around the home or work for a small fee as a labourer or farm worker.

It is extremely common to see girls working during the day, carrying rocks, digging holes and carrying water while their brothers are at school.

Achieving progress on female literacy is one of the Millennium Development Goals (MDGs) we are unlikely to reach by 2015. For every year a girl is kept in school above grade four, she gets married a year later and has a twenty per cent smaller family size.

The cycle next turns to eating practices. Young women need nutrients as their bodies grow and menstruation begins. Yet, in many families, women eat last and least. Young girls' bodies are not receiving sufficient nutrients to grow in a healthy way. They are anaemic and malnourished.

When a girl reaches puberty she can be married off. In parts of South Asia, sixty per cent of girls get married at the age of thirteen and are pregnant within the next year. To complete the Cycle of Malnutrition, this young, malnourished girl/woman gives birth to an underweight, malnourished child, and so, without intervention, the cycle continues, year in and year out, generation to generation.

RHEEMA – THE TYRANNY OF EARLY MARRIAGE

I will never forget meeting a young girl called Rheema in a village in Bangladesh. She was married at thirteen. The look of despair and resignation in her eyes is part of the reason I get up every day to do what I do. Rheema had attended school intermittently and was educated up to grade three. She had the most basic literacy skills and loved learning. A year before I met her, she was told that she was to be married to a man who was thirty-five. She did not want to get married and wanted to continue her education.

After her marriage, Rheema left her village to move about twenty kilometres away to live with her husband's family. Effectively she was removed from everything she knew – her family, friends and community – to live with strangers.

Now, marriage means sex. In Rheema's case, she was a thirteen-year-old girl being used sexually by her husband whenever he felt like it. She had no voice, no power to say no to sex or to use condoms to space out pregnancies. In a marriage of deep inequality, this scenario is nothing less than sexual slavery. As with Rheema, this situation is echoed in the lives of many women worldwide. I met Rheema nine months after she was married. She had just turned fourteen, and she was six months pregnant.

One of the biggest influences in marrying girls early in South Asia is dowries. The dowry is a horrible custom whereby the family of the bride is expected to pay the husband's family to marry their daughter. Although now illegal, it is still widely practised

It can bankrupt a family by creating a debt that lasts for a generation in some instances. The practice of paying another family to take your daughter off your hands is one reason why the birth of a daughter is so lamented. In this paradigm, the girl is seen as an economic burden. Not only is she another mouth to feed, she will cost the family dearly when it's time for her to be married. Because she will leave the village and the family, she is not considered to be an asset in any way. Thus, the imperative to have her educated is diminished. Instead, it is expected that she earn a small wage in the field to supplement the family income, rather than spending money on her schooling. She can't even play a role in the important burial rites for her parents. This framework of thinking considers that there is no upside in having a daughter.

A WOMAN'S DAY

In the countries where hunger still persists, a huge paradox exists. On one hand, societies entrust the birthing, raising, feeding and education of children to women. On the other hand, the same societies systematically deny these women the education, voice, freedom of movement and the opportunity to safely perform these duties. It's bizarre and profoundly unjust.

This is why the United Nations and other institutions conclude that one of the keys to solving world hunger and poverty is to empower women. It can be hard to comprehend the sort of drudgery and low status that hundreds of millions of women still face in the 21st century. While we might complain about our busy lives, consider a typical day for women like Meera living in developing countries.

MEERA – A COMMON LIFE

Meera rises first in her family, well before dawn. She goes outside to relieve herself, squatting in the field. During the whole day, this might be the only time she has to herself. There is no privacy for ablutions and, sadly, a woman can be assaulted while relieving herself.

Meera walks some distance to collect wood for the fire and lights it to prepare a small meal. She feeds the animals. She walks (often miles) to get water. Now consider what's actually involved in this one small sentence. Fetching water is tiresome and burdensome but essential part of any woman's day. Often women carry twenty litre containers – sometimes for miles. I dare you to carry this weight (about twenty kilograms) to your letter box and back! And before she even gets to take it home, she may have had to haul the water up by a bucket from the well. I've done this task myself: it's very heavy and the rope burns. It can take thirty or more attempts with the bucket to bring enough water from the well, and, unfortunately, it is often so cloudy and dirty that it isn't fit for human consumption. Of course, this water is still bought home to the family because even dirty water is better than none. Sadly, many women are unaware that the water needs to be boiled before it is fit to drink. Or, they may be aware of this but be unable to spare the wood for the fire to boil the water. (Hence, the prevalence of deaths by diarrhoea; all completely avoidable if safe drinking water were a priority.)

If Meera gets back from the well late, she may be beaten by her husband. Yes, it's true! It seems inconceivable that after walking miles to fetch water you might be beaten. However, if her husband thinks she has taken too long, he may beat her simply because he is suspicious of infidelity.

Meera then wakes her family, feeds her baby and serves a small breakfast (if there is some food, otherwise only tea). She prepares a meal for her husband's lunch and then goes to work in her small garden patch where she produces food for the family. Some days, she goes to the field where she works as a labourer, earning half the amount her husband earns.

At the end of the day, Meera walks to the well again to fetch more water. She then gathers firewood and begins cooking the evening meal for her family. She serves the meal first to her husband and he eats his fill. Then she feeds her sons, then her daughters and, lastly, if there is any remaining food, she eats. Finally, she breastfeeds her baby.

Meera cleans the pot and tidies up the hut. She may supervise her children's homework but, unfortunately, the lack of electricity can mean it is impossible to do any homework after dark. She retires to bed after everyone else and gets up the next morning to start this routine all over again.

What is incredible is that even with this daily life as a backdrop, women are rising up and challenging the old ways of doing things.

They're waking up every day and figuring out not just how they are going to feed their families, but how they will work to change the system within their communities.

Vision

To move toward creating a new reality, it is fundamental to have an idea of where you are headed. This is called 'vision'. It is the one key element that is evident in the vast majority of leadership success stories. Vision is the third step in the Nine Steps of Transformative Leadership process

The dictionary on my laptop computer defines vision as 'the ability to think about or plan the future with innovation, imagination or wisdom'. A compelling vision can enable people to achieve extraordinary change. Nothing big can be created without vision. It is often quoted that, 'Where there is no vision, the people perish.'

No matter where we live, a mindset of resignation can prevail. What do I mean by resignation? It's a feeling or belief that nothing will change. That regardless of what I do or don't do, it won't make any difference. This is especially true for people who live with hunger and poverty.

People quite reasonably think: hunger has always been here and always will be. They feel that no matter what they do, they will never be able to make enough to feed their family. Governments promise to help but often forget about the poor and hungry after the election is over. People feel there is no hope for a better future.

When the past has been a roadmap of failure, it often takes an intervention to create a new vision for the future. To have a vision of success when you have previously experienced betrayal or failure, takes courage. However, creating a vision that people can own and move forward with is crucial for change. It is the key criteria in being able to shift people's mindset.

This perception that people need to envision a future before they can initiate change is something I love about working with The Hunger Project. It is deeply honouring. Having hope for the future frees up people's innate capacity to transform their own lives and have a say in what they want. Envisioning the future is necessary in order to achieve your dreams, no matter who you are.

Creating a vision for the future – often in the face of huge obstacles – is in itself an act of leadership. It can be easier to be visionary when you've already experienced some success. But when you have minimal food, no education and this has been the situation throughout living memory, envisioning some other future seems almost impossible. It takes enormous courage to create a vision of a different life and then take even a small step to realise your goals

The stories in this chapter show us how having a bigger vision for our lives fundamentally changes us.

We see how Santosh Devi's fight to have women in her Indian village wear shoes empowered them to reclaim their dignity and elevated their status to being human. And how Parkhi – a non-literate agricultural worker – successfully campaigned in her village for young girls to be educated. And, finally, we read how local leaders like Nasim now realise the importance of acting with integrity and transforming their behaviour to benefit their whole community.

When creating a vision for your own life, ask yourself what outcomes you are seeking? Start with the end goal in mind. There is huge power in having clarity about what you want to accomplish, because it gives you the ability to focus and persevere to see your vision come to fruition.

THE POWER OF VISION

About twenty years ago, The Hunger Project Bangladesh created a process to enable the transformation of people's mindset from, 'I cannot' to 'I can' to 'We can'. It is called the Vision, Commitment and Action Workshop, and more than four million people have participated in it around the world. Taking part in this workshop is an incredibly profound experience, and I've been extremely lucky to sit in on them many times in Bangladesh and different countries in Africa.

The process starts with people sitting together as a group. People sit under a tree or in a circle in the centre of a village. The workshop is facilitated by a trained local volunteer leader, and the women are in the front to ensure their voices are heard. Some workshops are only a few people strong; others may have hundreds attending. In a few cases, they are held in a small hut with two women, one being the trainer and the other a local woman who cannot leave the walls of her home because of social constraints.

In the Vision, Commitment and Action workshop, people consider the idea of what their village could look like when free from hunger. This future is visualised, and people get specific. It might mean access to fresh water; children in school, men and women as friends, income generation that provides for the family, and safe sanitation, so children do not die of diarrhoea.

The workshop is intensely moving. I've sat in these sessions with communities and seen people weep as they dare to imagine a future that supports and honours them. People are inspired when a new world is opened to them – one they could not have imagined previously.

In the workshop, people begin to dream a different future into existence for themselves and their families. It reminds me of the way the activist and humanitarian, Helen Keller said she felt when the word 'w-a-t-e-r' was tapped into the palm of her hand. She said:

'That living word awakened my soul, gave it light, hope, joy, set it free! There were barriers still; it is true, but barriers that could in time be swept away.'

The next step is about 'commitment'. Once people are clear on their vision, they need to commit to make it happen. The result of your vision doesn't magically appear from out of the blue. Obstacles can happen. It takes concerted effort, collaboration, inner resolve and a willingness to see something through to the finish line. This is an important part of the process. People commit to bringing their vision into reality.

The 'action' part is looking at what the community can do to bring them a step closer to their vision. A key component is that this action must require no outside help or financial aid. This is a crucial part in shifting the mindset from dependency to self-reliance. When people see they have the capacity to create their own change, they take ownership. They don't need to wait for an outside agency – be it a governmental or non-governmental organisation (NGO) – to do it for them. This helps to break through the dependency mentality. People can have terrific ideas but fail to implement them because: 'It should be up to the government' or 'Charity should do it'. Sometimes people's plans do require some financial capital, but, in this process, they must also look to themselves and their communities to find or create the funding.

Likewise, there is an analytic component that is key to this process working successfully. Within the community, a range of priorities are put under scrutiny. Each idea is examined according to the following criteria: Can I do this? Can we do it as a community? Does it need a lot of money to implement? Do we need government support? Getting clear on what it's going to take to achieve the desired outcome has to happen before the community commits to taking the project on.

As a principle, the first actions require no outside financial or other help. Take, for instance, sanitation. This is a problem in countries where people defecate in fields and where women have no safe place to go to the toilet for fear of assault. The action communities decide to undertake – a vision around safe sanitation – might be to dig and construct three latrines in the next six weeks. The community mobilises to build, dig and install those latrines.

If education is the number one priority, community members who have some literacy may commit to teaching a class every afternoon for two hours. It is amazing to be in a village where a circle of people gather under a tree from 4.00 pm until 6.00 pm in the afternoon to learn literacy from a couple of the educated villagers. They may use a stick and the sand on the ground as their pen and paper, but they do learn.

Sometimes a community income generation project might be the priority. In Bangladesh, a silted pond can be de-silted, allowing clean water to be captured and making a perfect environment for fish farming. To create this outcome, everyone in the community gives labour or money to have the pond de-silted. The result is a fish farming activity that provides protein for the community and seed capital for new projects.

One of the biggest impacts of the Vision, Commitment and Action Workshops is the shift in people's thinking about themselves, their community and what is possible. A switch seems to turn on inside the community. Once the villagers have accomplished something together using their own resources, they see that more things are possible. They are keen to consolidate this progress with new activities that will help them to achieve their vision. Real momentum is gained, and soon many different projects are in motion as people work to bring their vision into fruition. It all becomes possible!

People set broader visions along with time frames, and then design campaigns of action to bring about change. I have been to villages where there is a shared commitment to achieve one hundred per cent literacy in the next twelve months, or to have child marriage eradicated within a similar period of time.

Big changes are possible and achievable from the seeds of small ideas and dreams.

Things to think about: SHIFTING THE MINDSET

❧ Changing people's mindset isn't magic. It's deep work that includes the social element, as well as the personal. There are social beliefs and assumptions at play that shape and are shaped by the personal mindset. Bringing awareness to both the social and the individual mindset is the first place to start in order to transform them.

❧ Our mindsets are often unconscious for us, because 'that's the way it is'. We can bring consciousness to how we think and act. When we don't understand what drives our behaviour, we may live a life of reaction and justification, coming up with lots of excuses for why things are they way are and why we can never change.

❧ If you do the necessary inner work to understand and illuminate what makes you feel or react in a certain way, then you can master your responses.

SANTOSH DEVI – POWER OF SYMBOLS

Some people really love shoes, and women are stereotypically known to be obsessed with them. Carrie Bradshaw, Imelda Marcos – I'll stop there. Whether we are male or female, the shoes we wear can be a powerful way of expressing ourselves. Although shoes are practical items, they can also be a source of creative expression or a statement about your mood, your style or even your income bracket. With this in mind, it was revelatory for me to meet Santosh Devi and hear her story centred on shoes.

Santosh lived in a remote tribal community in India. She attended training sessions for women's leaders at which I was an observer. She seemed to be in her late forties, but she was probably much younger. In rural India it can be hard to tell the actual age of a woman as hot sun, lack of water and nutrition, and drudgery all combine to accelerate ageing.

I was sitting in a circle at the women's training session and leaned in closer to hear her story. The area she came from was extremely hard on women. Women had no rights. Girls were not even allowed to be educated. Although barring girls from attending school is illegal and against the Indian constitution, in her area the community banned girls from attending school. Santosh herself had not received any formal education.

Discrimination against women and girls was endemic. One way in which discrimination was enforced was by banning women from wearing shoes. It was actually forbidden for women to wear anything on their feet; not even slippers. Now in some parts of India, the wearing of shoes is linked to respect. For instance, if a lower caste man or woman walks past a higher caste person's house, it is not uncommon to see them take off their shoes just before reaching the house, put the shoes on their head as they walk past, and then put their shoes back on once they have passed by.

However, in Santosh's village this outward display of deference was taken to a humiliating extreme: women were expected to always be barefoot. The visual symbolism of this is hard to escape. Unlike other animals, humans are the only creatures who wear shoes: shoes keep us above the dust, the dirt, and painful sharp rocks and stones. The fact that every woman in her village didn't wear shoes conferred a sub-human status to women and girls alike, exacerbating their subjugation within the community. This custom had become internalised as the norm.

After Santosh was trained by The Hunger Project, her world widened. She learned that women could be leaders. She understood that women have the same rights as men – including the right to choose their own clothing. She also learned that, under the Indian constitution, girls have a right to be educated. She became impassioned to bring her community into line with India's law.

As a first step, Santosh raised her voice against the edict banning women from wearing shoes. Santosh herself started wearing shoes while walking in the village. She went from door to door trying to convince women to wear shoes. She tried explaining the harmful effects of not wearing them. She requested that all the women attending the village meetings wear shoes.

Initially, the men (and some women) reacted very negatively to her ideas. They felt threatened. They tried to pressure her by calling her names, saying she was mad, out of her senses and an animal. This backlash occurred because she advised the village to go against the long-held customs and traditions. In the early stages, the men boycotted the village meetings. However, with the help and support of some women and girls, Santosh continued her struggle and at last succeeded in convincing everybody that women and girls had the right to wear shoes.

The next project in Santosh's vision was educating girls. She approached the local council about allowing girls to attend the existing boys-only school. There were many reasons given against this, all of which were thinly veiled attempts to deter her from achieving her goal. Some people said that it was not safe for girls to be in a school with boys. Others speculated that parents would never allow their girls to mix with boys. There were rumours that girls' reputations would be ruined if they attended a school with boys.

Santosh stood firm in her beliefs. She knew she had Indian law on her side. Rather than upsetting the existing arrangement of the boys-only school, she approached the government and lobbied them to build a school for girls. This necessitated many trips into the nearest town, which was two hours away on foot. She persuasively and persistently put the village case forward to the bureaucrats and eventually received the funds to build a school for girls.

The school is now in operation and has more than two hundred and fifty girls in attendance. Female teachers are paid by the government. More girls are enrolling, and Santosh is working to get the school buildings extended. Having a school dedicated to girls' education was such a positive change for the whole community.

Santosh shows us that symbols are important. Her fight to have women wear shoes was not merely about the shoes. It was about reclaiming dignity and respect for women and elevating their status to that of being properly human. The nature of the community changed significantly as a result of women wearing shoes.

Things to think about: POWER OF SYMBOLS

❧ While Santosh's story might shock us with its blatant sexist message of banning all women and girls from wearing footwear, we have similar symbols in our own culture that reinforce existing power structures. Symbols are one of the earliest methods of communication – even pre-verbal. What are some of the symbols you recognise that constrain, diminish or humiliate, and how can you set about dismantling them?

❧ We recognise where power resides from visual cues. The layout of offices, the clothes we wear and the labels all tell us something. Who speaks in meetings? Where do people with different positions in an organisation sit? Are you the only woman walking into a board meeting where men predominate? All of these send strong visual messages that remind us where we fit in. Be aware of the messages you are sending or buying into through unsaid, but visible, mediums.

PARKHI – COMMITMENT FINDS A WAY

One of the many insights I've gained from my work with The Hunger Project is the concept of being fully committed.

Parkhi is an agricultural worker from a tribal area in India where girls did not go to school – ninety per cent of women in this region were non-literate. It was generally agreed that girls were needed to herd goats and make fuel cakes out of cow dung.

As an elected women's representative leader in the Indian local council system, Parkhi was trained by The Hunger Project. She realised the power for change within the next generation would only occur if girls could get an education. Even though she hadn't had that opportunity herself, Parkhi was determined that other girls would.

Parkhi passionately campaigned in her village for the value, necessity and right of girls to be educated. The issue wasn't that there was no school available, as we have seen in some other stories. Rather, it was that parents did not feel it was necessary for their daughters to attend school, especially when they needed them for manual labour.

Parkhi went door to door canvassing about the importance of girls' education. She shared with me how she spoke to families constantly, never giving up on her vision. Eventually she created some real momentum around the concept that it's important for girls to be literate and numerate. Parkhi was very animated while she recounted the steps she took and the objections she'd had to overcome. As a result of her leadership, forty girls in that area now go to school. Forty lives have been changed forever because of what she did.

I asked her who now looked after the goats? She responded, 'You find new ways. Others take care of them or goats are bought home. Herding goats can be achieved through other means, but girls cannot be educated through another process.'

I was profoundly moved by this clarity. Parkhi's logic and reasoning is an incredible demonstration of the importance of disregarding all options other than the one you are committed to. In doing so, smaller issues get resolved.

We find so many reasons not to do the big stuff (educating girls) because we get caught up in our excuses/challenges (herding goats). When we commit to something big, all other issues get handled in the face of that bigger commitment.

Things to think about: COMMITMENT

❧ Parkhi's story demonstrates that when we commit to something big, the smaller details sort themselves out.

❧ We all make excuses as to why we don't achieve the things we know we could. This is our version of 'herding goats'. What is your version of sending your girls to school? Can you find another way to 'get your goats herded'?

❧ Can you create a large enough vision for your life that you will seek ways to resolve your current obstacles and challenges? Rather than settling for the way things are, dream big. In that space, the things that seem to constrain us get addressed.

NASIM – IMPORTANCE OF TRANSPARENCY

Mohammed Nasim is a local government official in Bangladesh who was skimming a bit of money off the top. He was extremely open about it: one might say disarmingly transparent. Almost everyone in government circles did it – this is probably the reason why international watchdog Transparency International used to rate Bangladesh as one of the most corrupt countries in the world.

Nasim is not an inherently bad person. In fact, he is a likeable bloke – charming and tolerant of his daughters' education. Skimming a bit of money off the top is just how you get ahead in Bangladesh. It is not personal. However, the cost to the community is high. As a result of money being creamed off by local government officials, services budgeted for the poor such as water and schools don't eventuate. The net effects of this behaviour are catastrophic for the less fortunate.

Nasim attended the Animators Training. The Animators Training is a powerful four-day leadership programme that more than one hundred thousand local people have completed in Bangladesh. People confront and transform their own mindset of resignation and dependency and, most importantly, gain skills in unlocking their innate leadership abilities. It's very moving to see people commit firstly to themselves to ending their own hunger, and secondly, to supporting their community in collectively ending its hunger. Through the Animators training, people are also then equipped to lead the Vision, Commitment and Action workshop.

During this training, Nasim got in touch with a deeper purpose for his life: namely service to his community. While it had seemed advantageous to him to have more of life's perks, he now understood that it didn't work for the community as a whole. This situation, in fact, limited the quality of life that his family enjoyed. If you have ever been to Bangladesh and witnessed the unworkability of local infrastructure and services such as electricity, sewerage or transport you would know what I mean. There are constant power outages, strikes and general disorder. No one wants to live under these conditions if it can be avoided.

As a result of his new perspective, Nasim instituted open budget sessions at his local government meetings. I was privileged to attend the first one. There were about four hundred villagers crammed into a small hall. It was steamy, and many people were trying to find room to sit in the limited space. Two or three people attempted to squeeze onto a single chair. No one was complaining. Instead, there was a rapt silence and stillness as every line item from the local government budget was read aloud. People heard how much was spent on pens, tea, roadworks, etc. The whole community was present, and you could have heard a pin drop. One old man cried. He stood up and said, his voice full of emotion, 'I'm eighty years old and I never thought I would live to see this happen.'

Everyone present discussed priorities for government spending for the next six months. Accountability was present and the people had a say in how their money was to be spent.

Other than his normal salary, Nasim no longer profits financially from his government position. Instead, his community is flourishing. Children are mostly a healthy weight, and he is running a programme in partnership with The Hunger Project to achieve one hundred per cent literacy.

There are now many unions (local government councils) across Bangladesh's sixty-four districts that now have these open budget meetings. They are led by leaders like Nasim who are choosing to live with a greater vision. They think about what they are doing, rather than unconsciously playing the system. They are driving the movement for transformative change within their society.

Things to think about: TRANSPARENCY

- When you know a system is not working, it takes courage to identify new pathways, take action and ultimately create a new system. This is especially true when there is no immediate reward.

- Nasim was able to see that not only he would benefit from being more transparent, so would his entire community. Are you transparent? What are you worrying about hiding? Are you so busy hiding that your real self fails to show up?

- Sometimes we unwittingly collude with others to justify certain behaviours or beliefs. We might surround ourselves with people who make us feel better about not giving our best. Daring to do things differently might challenge your normal peer group. What accountability structure can you set up to support you in your efforts to live a bigger life?

Personal Responsibility

Taking responsibility for your life and accepting that you are the only one that can create the change you seek is a theme throughout this book. It is the common characteristic amongst our *Unlikely Leaders* and forms the fourth step in the Nine Steps of Transformative Leadership.

Rather than considering responsibility as a burden, we could reframe it as the gateway to our being agents of change and transformation. When we are responsible for how our life unfolds, we discover real freedom and power. We move from being the victim of circumstance to being a leader. Power and freedom come from not fleeing responsibility but, instead, embracing it and stepping up.

It is easy to blame others when times get tough in our lives. It's also easier to live in hope that someone might save us, or that things will change without having to take any action. But when you step up, things happen! Instead of living in a place of despair, or resigned to things never changing, you move into a place of personal power.

This is the essence and design of personal responsibility – it's up to you, and no one else is going to, or even can, make these changes in your life for you.

It's a powerful principle to live by that 'organisations or countries don't change, people do'. In psychology, this is referred to as 'internal locus of control versus external locus of control'. Internal locus of control means you are self-directed, which is the essence of personal responsibility. External locus of control is when you feel things happen to you all the time and you have no say in, or power over, what happens.

Transforming our mindset – shifting from external to internal locus of control – is critical to every human endeavour. It's about owning our ability to make change and play the leading role in our own life. This is as true for a developed nation like Australia as it is for a person living in a village in Bangladesh or Ethiopia.

In this chapter, we will meet Kenchamma, who assumed responsibility through her elected leadership role and, despite harsh opposition, demonstrated resilience by continuing to fight for reforms in her community. Plus Rheeana, from a Bangladesh village, who, resourcefully, was able change people's attitudes to prevent young girls marrying too young. And, finally, young Deborah, who at five years of age had the courage to get up in front of a large crowd and speak out to advocate for social reform.

These stories are all the more remarkable because the conditions people find themselves in are so harsh and so entrenched. Yet people's discovery of their own agency – their own ability to lead and have a say – produces incredible outcomes.

KENCHAMMA – RESILIENT FOR CHANGE

Kenchamma is a non-literate Dalit (most disadvantaged) caste woman from south India. She never received an education; therefore, she works as an occasional farm labourer when work is available. Most people would not look at her and think of her as the key to ending hunger in her village.

Nearly twenty years ago, an extraordinary amendment to the Indian constitution meant that one third of all seats at the local council, called 'panchayat', were reserved for women. This meant that, following elections, more than one million women across India were voted in as elected women representatives with a mandate to govern in their villages. Kenchamma was one of these women. Yet, like many others, she was not yet conscious of the difference she could make in her elected position.

Kenchamma hadn't chosen or decided to stand for election. Her thumbprint was used by her male family members to register her. If elected, she was expected to step aside and let her family make all the decisions for her. She was to be a proxy for the male members of her family, as they believed her vote could be manipulated to suit them. No one thought she would even attend meetings. She was subjugated by her family and had no voice and no standing in the community. It was expected that she would ratify all the male family members' decisions. Given this situation, how could she lead?

The Hunger Project has trained one hundred thousand elected women village leaders across India, and Kenchamma was one of them. After learning about her duty as an elected leader and her constitutional rights, she became excited about what changes she could achieve for her village, which still had no electricity or clean water.

Kenchamma was never given information about when the council meetings were held; however, after working with The Hunger Project, she made it her business to become informed. Kenchamma

53

sought out the information and attended her first council meeting as an elected woman leader. The meeting took place in a small hall, and she took a seat at the table.

Then something startling happened. Kenchamma was immediately surrounded by the other council members, picked up and physically thrown out of the building on to the street outside. The chair she had been sitting on was thrown into the street as well. Finally, they picked up the table they were all sitting at and threw that outside, too. She was told that if she must attend meetings she should stand outside on the step and conduct her business from there, so she did not pollute them.

Think for a minute how you might react if this happened to you. Remarkably, she did not let this episode faze her. For the next two years of her council tenure, she turned up to every meeting and participated in proceedings from the step just outside the building. After two years, she was finally permitted into the hall. During her fourth year of office, Kenchamma came into her own as a leader and as a voice for the poor. Her many achievements included ensuring the supply of electricity to all four hundred huts in her village – something never before attempted. She also secured fresh water for her community. Government water programmes were available which no one had previously applied for. Kenchamma made sure she found out about these programmes and worked hard to get budget approval to commence work on the projects. She succeeded, and due to her efforts, water pipes were laid and connected into her village.

Kenchamma wrote the book on never giving up – without ever becoming literate! She kept turning up and insisting something be done about her village's circumstances.

While it may not have been her goal, Kenchamma's far-sighted quest eventually wore away the social armour of her status-driven colleagues, enabling them to show real respect for her endeavours. She ended up becoming the president of her village council.

Kenchamma demonstrates to us that if we are going to create change, we need to be resilient.

Things to think about: RESILIENCE

- ❧ Kenchamma was extremely humble. Her efforts were never about her – she stood up for her people. She was selfless. How often do we make every little thing about us?

- ❧ Kenchamma had every reason to complain about how humiliating it was to be treated so unfairly. She could have used the excuse, 'I gave it my best shot, but I can't work with these people!' No one would have disagreed with her about that.

- ❧ The other council members did not welcome Kenchamma, but she did not get caught up in their issues or obstinate viewpoints. She simply focused on the difference she would make. Kenchamma's story is a powerful lesson in self-worth. It's interesting that we often base our self-worth on what others think and on the power others give us. Kenchamma shows us that we can create change where we are right now. She shows us that we are each fully equipped to do what needs to be done.

- ❧ Kenchamma had a burning desire for change in her village. Was she initially embarrassed? Probably. Did she have second thoughts, even if fleeting? I know I would have! However, she did not dwell on this. The idea of a better life for her village propelled her forward. Kenchamma's vision and purpose were bigger than any personal slights she may have felt

RHEEANA – FROM LITTLE THINGS, BIG THINGS GROW

I met a young woman a number of years ago who you might think had no resources. Rheeana was from a small village in Bangladesh. She had limited education and no standing within her community. She was just a simple village woman.

Rheeana came into contact with The Hunger Project and attended a Vision, Commitment and Action Workshop. During the workshop, Rheeana learned that it was possible to eliminate hunger and poverty in her village and that she could be part of the process to bring about this change. Rheeana understood that if things were to change there was no point waiting for a miracle; it would have to start with her. This excited and intrigued her.

Rheeana joined a self-help group started by Hunger Project volunteers. This group brought women together to offer support and help each other improve their situations. In Rheeana's group, in lieu of a members' fee, each woman committed to putting aside a fistful of rice before cooking their one meal a day. To us this may seem like a small thing, but for these women it was a substantial investment. Often the only daily meal for their families was a bowl of rice topped with some fried onion and chilli. Over the course of a week, each woman saved a small mound of rice. The women then brought this rice to the weekly self-help group meeting where it was pooled to be sold at the market. This resource provided the basis for a small capital fund which was available to lend each week to one of the members in order to start up an income-generating activity.

When it was Rheeana's turn to receive the money, she was so thrilled! She had always dreamed of having a small poultry business, so she used her money to buy a couple of chickens. Over time, those two hens multiplied and Rheeana soon made enough money selling eggs and chickens to support herself. She then started to think of expanding her small enterprise. She sold some hens and bought a small cow. She sold the milk and made yogurt in her little dairy business. With economic empowerment came confidence.

Rheeana started to think about how she could help others in her village. During the time she was building her small business, she heard that her twelve-year-old female cousin was getting married. From her training as a volunteer leader in her village, Rheeana was aware of the consequences of early marriage and how detrimental it was to the health of the girl, the family and the community. Rheeana decided that this marriage would not happen while she lived and breathed. She set about trying to stop the marriage.

Rheeana first approached the family, who were in the process of preparing the wedding feast, to demand that the marriage be stopped, citing the child's age as the reason. The family refused and lied about the girl's age, saying she was eighteen. When Rheeana demanded to see the birth certificate, she was marched out of the hut.

Rheeana then went to see the Imam – the religious leader in the village. She told the Imam that the girl was underage, and he must not go ahead with the ceremony. The Imam went to talk to the family, but could not persuade them to abandon the marriage. He resignedly informed Rheeana that it was to take place. He told her there was nothing that he could do to prevent the marriage from taking place.

Rheeana then mobilised a dozen women from her self-help group and went to the police. This is a bold move in a country where corruption is rife and police are not normally sympathetic to 'domestic' issues. However, Rheeana was formidable in her focus to stop the child's marriage. In the end, the police went to the hut and stopped the marriage.

Rheeana was not someone you would normally think of as a leader. Yet she surprised people repeatedly. Through her partnership and activity with the self-help group, Rheeana won other people's trust and confidence, so much so that this group supported her efforts to convince the police to prevent the marriage. She worked with others; she recognised that any sizeable endeavour can't be accomplished alone.

As a footnote, I met Rheeana about two years after this incident. I also met the family and the young girl, who was now fourteen. Interestingly, the girl's parents grumbled to me about their daughter not being married – evidence that it can take a while for people's mindsets to change and that not everyone welcomes the changes. This is true in any group. However, this young girl was still unmarried and still in school!

Rheeana is the very definition of an *Unlikely Leader*. She didn't have the advantages that you might think are required to make things happen. Yet she was able to create change in the status quo.

Things to think about: BEING RESOURCEFUL

- ❧ Rheeana reminds us that we are all sitting on a mountain of value and resources. What resources do you have? How can you uncover more? How can you leverage what you have? How can this be of service to others?

- ❧ Think about Rheeana if you feel you don't have enough resources to make a difference – whether it's time, money or energy. We all have resources – both inner and outer. Rheeana collaborated with others – and so she was able to multiply her own resources. She was disciplined. She started small but grew, both in her business and as a leader.

- ❧ Rheeana created a vision for her life that encompassed more than herself. She could have just kept her focus on her business, yet she did not.

❧ Our lives are not just about us. Ask yourself, 'What is my legacy? How can I help others while I build my life/business?'

ISHITA – SOCIAL ACTION CROSSES BORDERS

A number of years ago, I met Ishita, who lived in a Bangladeshi village near the Indian border. She was a lively, curious twelve-year-old girl, but she lived in an area with a high incidence of trafficking girls across the border for prostitution and sex slavery in India. Girls like Ishita are often tricked into going. In other circumstances, parents sell them for financial gain. Sometimes families genuinely believe they are giving their daughters a better chance, but all too often this transaction is used as a way of making some extra money and ridding themselves of the problems of girls and dowries. At the time of my visit, my own daughter was twelve.

On a bus back to Dhaka, the sun was setting, and the sky was beautiful. I fell into that almost trance-like state you can get on long road trips. I started reflecting on what we trade for money. I could not stop thinking about how widespread the practice of trafficking of young girls like Ishita was in these villages.

I started extrapolating; thinking of all the different things we do for money, and how we turn a blind eye to the way things get done to maintain profit. Surely, if we got to the root of what drives this behaviour, we might be able to change it. It is convenient to see situations like sex trafficking as an aberration of a country like Bangladesh or a certain subset of evil people. However, this industry is in part driven by a complete unconsciousness around money and survival that implicates us all. Sometimes human beings will literally do anything for money.

I began to consider what my family did to make money and what other people within my country did to make money. While I know that no one reading this book has sold their daughters into sexual slavery, or subjected their children to underage work environments, there are many ways we compromise on what we know to be right –

for money. We may work for a pay cheque in industries that pollute. We may invest in companies that knowingly exploit workers for the dividends we'll receive. We may work long hours for extra consumables while missing out on meaningful family time. We may buy goods that were produced in sweatshops or cheap timber furniture that has come from old growth forests, simply to save money.

During my drive, I tried to comprehend what it must be like to be a village girl who is tricked and sent away from her family for a life of prostitution and slavery. This horrific practice was happening to hundreds of these young girls every day. What could be done about it?

Again, a large part of the solution lies with the people affected by the situation. Near the Indian/Bangladeshi border, local people were trained and mobilised, alerting their own community to these issues. Their focus was on shifting people's thinking by first developing an awareness and appreciation for the value of girls and women. Girls must be considered an asset and worth investing in.

Eight years after this trip, I again visited the same village and heard numerous stories about how girls were no longer being sent across the border to India to be sex workers. The practice had stopped. The community had initiated door-to-door campaigns to break the silence on what really happens to girls once they leave their families and move to India. They also took a stand to stamp out dowry – the insidious custom of paying the husband's family to marry your daughter, which can financially cripple a family and makes girls the focus of financial strife.

A causative effect of this change is that families of men were now not accepting dowry payments. In fact, when I asked young men if they would take dowry, the look on their faces was one of complete disdain. They were offended by the question. One village has been *one hundred per cent* dowry free for a few years. This reorientation of village values took time and sustained effort, but was successful in preventing girls from being trafficked into India from this area.

This campaign was coupled with income-generating opportunities that gave families other alternatives for making money. One such income-generating activity involved the entire community de-silting a fishpond in order to grow fingerlings (small fish fry), thereby providing grown fish to sell. Without exception, everyone in the community contributed either money or labour. The fish were harvested and provided protein for the villagers, as well as income to be shared amongst everyone.

It is clarifying and empowering to reorient our values around what types of activities we will do to make money, as well as how we spend it. We are witnessing this happening all over the world with movements urging people to downsize by working less, buying less and being conscious of the ethicality of the supply chain that brings us our goods. People are also recognising that they can use some of their money to make a difference in the world through astutely giving to causes that count and movements that matter. Such money is an investment in a new future.

Personal responsibility can be assumed for global issues too. It's always good to be open to the possibility of change. It's easy to look at someone else or some other country and point out what they are doing wrong. It's harder to see ourselves as a microcosm of a world that is full of so many injustices.

Things to think about: SOCIAL ACTION AND MONEY

❧ What would we do for money? What do we do for money? Give some thought to how you earn your money, including the investments you make. Does it represent your real values? Have a look and see whether there are some things you will turn a blind eye to if it means that you'll make a profit.

❧ Seeing the changes in these villages over the years, I think about the work The Hunger Project does to reinvent our relationship to money. Money can energise and harness our potential to make a big difference in the world. It can also remain in the grip of our consumer malaise. Changing this relationship to money is challenging work. In wealthier countries – like the region near the Bangladeshi border – we must all be conscious about the choices we make around money.

YOUNG DEBORAH – COURAGE TO SPEAK

Finding courage to speak up can be a lifetime journey, especially for women. For years, women have been culturally conditioned to not voice their opinion. They have no say in village meetings or the decision making that affects their lives. Until very recently, this was true across the whole world. Today, in some areas, women may not leave the confines of their hut. I've been to a number of places where you can walk through the local streets or market and not see a single woman. They are invisible in so many ways.

Because women are not encouraged to speak, violence can be used to keep them in their place. More than once I have seen acid stored in a family's home. It may never be used, but it nonetheless serves as a threat and a reminder of what might happen if the woman is deemed to be out of line. This can even be the case for something as innocent as being watched by a man at the market. More than fifteen hundred cases of acid throwing causing disfigurement occur each year. It is pernicious.

Nevertheless, women are starting to come forward and express their opinions. In village meetings, in front of the whole community, women's voices are being heard. Imagine standing in front of your community and speaking about the need for a school bus so your daughters can travel to school unmolested. Or demanding to see the list of families below the poverty line from a government official, to ensure the right people are receiving staples such as rice from the government, instead of the list being corrupted. Imagine speaking up to your husband, insisting that money goes to the children's school fees and not his entertainment.

Maybe you are reading this and thinking – well, these people have the impetus to change as they have the most to gain. Well, then, think again. Human nature does not work like this. Often we get so enmeshed in 'the way things are' that we are simply not able to imagine anything different. When you have been working so hard just to subsist; when you are anaemic, beaten, hungry or burying children, you are focusing on trying to survive another day, not pro-actively envisioning a new future. Such ideas initially seem so far from the realm of reality they might as well be fantasy.

A woman speaking out is crucial for improvement in a community's life. The biggest step forward is the transition from an attitude of resignation to that of possibility. That is: moving from 'I can't' to 'I can' to 'We can'. Within the community, this change manifests in the way in which women are perceived. In other words, it involves a shift from them being considered as 'beasts of burden' to productive community members.

This change has a powerful effect on the next generation. A few years ago, I witnessed an inspiring event involving Deborah – a young Malawian girl from one of the Epicentres (a facility built by the lo-cal people for community interaction, microfinance, healthcare and education) The Hunger Project has mobilised. Deborah was no more than five years of age and she was speaking with a microphone in front of a crowd of people. She was following in her mother's foot-steps in the best possible way. In her world, it was appropriate to talk and be heard! We all enjoyed the fact that, for this young girl, speak-ing in front of the whole village was now the new norm.

Things to think about: SPEAKING OUT

❧ Speaking out has its challenges for all of us, no matter where we live. How often do we not speak out when there's something that needs to be said? If we are at work and see things that are not right, it takes courage to speak out. Sometimes we say nothing because we think either we'll lose our friends, or job, or we think we can't make a difference.

❧ Speaking out is different from complaining. Complaining is whining about something to someone who can't influence the situation in any way. It's half-hearted and inauthentic. Speaking out takes commitment. It's about provoking something different to happen. People know where you stand when you speak out.

❧ Speaking up means airing something that is unpopular but needs to be said. Sometimes we say nothing and hope for the best. Speaking up is a true act of courage.

Collective Power

Regardless of how ready for action, inspired by vision, and motivated for change you are, you can only achieve so much on your own. An old proverb says: 'If you want to travel fast, travel alone. If you want to travel far, travel with others.' By working together with others – the fifth step in the Nine Steps of Transformative Leadership – we build lasting change both in our own lives and in our communities.

With the support of people committed to the same goal as us, we can achieve so much more than on our own. We might stumble individually at a roadblock, but with a coalition we can break through. I have seen this continually around the world. Courage and strength of heart is found by joining with others. When you take on a big challenge, and it looks like you might succeed, a backlash can occur. This can be hard to deal with. On your own, you might give up. You might take the opposition to heart. You might feel threatened. With collective power, you are not alone. You can build momentum. This is how movements grow. They make large changes possible.

When a group of people makes the decision to work together, something magical happens that is more than the sum of the parts. The result is twofold. There's the power of solidarity, as demonstrated by a woman in India who held up her pen as a metaphor for a leader and said to me, 'One pen they can break, five pens together they cannot break'. She's right. Then there's the power of shared values which, when combined with a transparent flow of information, plus high levels of trust and communication, can result in substantial changes. The mind shift can be expressed as, 'With others, we can do more'. The beauty of collective power is that, when others take on board the new ways of thinking, it can affect a whole society and start extraordinary social change.

This fifth step of collective power demonstrates the movement from, 'I can't' to 'I can' to 'we can' that is at the heart of this book. In this chapter, we will read about the power of the collective and how working in unison leads to amazing results. This is exemplified in the stories of the coffee growers of Uganda, and in Hena and her self-help group working to support other women in her Bangladeshi village.

COFFEE COOPERATIVE

Many of us love our morning coffee.

One of the places where coffee is grown is in the high, rich, fertile soils of Uganda. You may know about Uganda due to the notoriety of a former president, Idi Amin, who earned the name 'Butcher of Uganda' throughout his brutal reign of terror from 1971 to 1979. Communities were literally torn apart as neighbours became enemies and, in some cases, turned against each other in the most violent ways.

We have all experienced trusting someone in the past, only to have it come back to bite us. Sometimes we decide to trust anew but, in some cases, it may seem safer to not trust again and so we decide to rely only on ourselves. This dynamic took on a whole new dimension in Uganda. Deep divisiveness became a hallmark of communities who suffered under the dictator's regime. One of the enduring legacies of this time was lack of trust within communities: people decided it was safer to 'go it alone'. Their individual success would see them rise and fall on their own capacity. In light of Uganda's recent history, this made perfect sense. When your livelihood and the survival of your family is at stake, you are unlikely to trust anyone when there is the risk of everything being taken from you.

There are enormous practical as well as emotional repercussions to a lack of trust. One such consequence was that Ugandans grew their crops individually and sold them individually. This meant that every coffee grower in the village sold their coffee to a middleman for a lower price than they could have received had they banded together. Even though they knew they would get a better price as a collective rather than as individuals, they were too fearful to trust others.

One of the benefits of The Hunger Project's approach to solving problems is that people learn to renew trust in each other. In bringing Ugandan communities together to work to a common purpose, it became clear that it was important to figure out a way to get more money as a group for their crops. One outcome was the formation of a coffee collective, whereby price was negotiated and delivery taken – together. People now receive a much higher and fairer price for their product, and the labour involved.

This story about coffee is a deceptively simple example of the subtle but powerful benefits from this human component in ending hunger. Creating trust and respect where there was previously fear and disillusionment initiates healing. Due to shared effort, things start to work in new and beneficial ways. Sustained peace is more likely. People now have too much invested in their community to abandon trust and risk alienation. Trust becomes a courageous, healing act of leadership.

Things to think about: TRUST

- Issues around trust and respect abound in all walks of life, even without a horrific war forcing people to behave in a certain way. For some of us, stoicism is a default setting. The upside is that we don't have to rely on others – well, as little as possible. The downside is that it's harder to leverage our business if decisions and activities are solely driven and controlled by us as individuals, because partnering with someone else is seen as too risky. The same dynamic can spill into our private lives where, for some people, even love is considered to be too risky.

- The power of meaningful partnerships can't be overestimated. Letting go of past hurts, or those times when something didn't work out, may necessitate a leap of faith and some courage. But it is the only route to success. Trust is not something earned by the recipient; it is an act of generosity that rewards itself.

HENA – GROWING MONEY

It is reasonable to think that people living in hunger and poverty lack money or resources. I used to think that as well.

Even in the world's poorest communities, money is in circulation. People need to buy bare necessities. Medicine needs to be paid for; so does education, because even when the government provides free schooling, uniforms and books still need to be bought. It is true that these people do not have much, but when money and resources are viewed expansively and imaginatively, it is possible to break free from hunger and poverty.

All over the world I've seen thousands of examples of people successfully growing their small assets. It starts with a belief that change is possible, and crucially, an understanding of, 'I cannot grow without you.' Reciprocity is key. It encompasses the awareness that, 'For me to create opportunity, I need to help you with yours.'

Worldwide, self-help groups are a terrific example of the power of working together for mutual community benefits. Across south Asia and Africa, a self-help group is typically comprised of twenty to thirty members – all women from one village. They meet regularly (usually once a week) to learn from each other how they can improve their lives and the lives of their families. Sometimes information is exchanged on strategies to increase wellbeing such as washing hands with soap after defecating, or the need to breastfeed exclusively for the first six months.

A self-help group can also be an informal credit provider. Members pool their resources together to provide capital for small business ventures. Each woman agrees to pay a small amount each week to the meeting (a membership fee). When enough money is collected, one member can borrow this amount for an income-generating project. Over a period of time, that money is repaid and then can be borrowed again. Meanwhile, membership fees continue to accrue and, in time, multiple loans can be disbursed to members. This is a beautiful example of how to think resourcefully and leverage the power of networks.

In developing countries, women are extremely entrepreneurial and savvy. They set up all kinds of businesses to support their families. Sometimes their business grows large enough to employ others. While visiting Gaibandha in Bangladesh I met Hena who started with a few taka (local money) from her women's group and over time built a small hand-sewing business from this minuscule amount of money. After a few years she had saved enough to purchase a sewing machine which she used to make boxes. She now sells these boxes to shops to package their wares and employs five people in her business. Hena did not have the money to start this enterprise on her own, but through the power of a network of others she had sufficient capital to start the process.

A life-changing innovation I've seen in some villages is creating an insurance net for the group members. In addition to the small membership fee, women bring along some uncooked rice. This is then pooled and stored in a large plastic bucket. The rice is kept as 'insurance' for times when/if a member needs money urgently for medicine or some other emergency. In this case, the rice is sold and given to the member to help them.

Members of the village's self-help groups are able to view their own resources more expansively over time. Through collective action, they have found a way to grow both their capital and their confidence.

Things to think about: GROWING MONEY

❖ Rather than guard and hold onto what you have, try collaborating and partnering to build growth.

❖ We can all suffer from a mindset of scarcity, where we believe we don't have enough. These self-help groups show that small change, used strategically can create big opportunities. Thinking innovatively and including others opens up a world of opportunity not available on your own.

❖ When we think expansively about what we have, it can multiply. And when this relates to new thinking, it has the same effect, particularly when others come on board. It is the catalyst for great change.

EVOLUTION OF A TRADITION

It is infinitely easier to recognise someone else's blind spot or issues instead of your own. It is easy to see where your kids or your spouse have gone wrong; to be bemused at the decisions friends have made; to notice dysfunctional dynamics in another family. The sense of the absurdity of life is never clearer than when visiting a country or a society other than your own. Of course, that's exactly what strikes them too, when they see you …

Resisting our tendencies to pre-judge is, I believe, one of the keys to achieving extraordinary results. We can't help but judge; it's part of human nature. Therefore, it requires restraint and self-discipline to suspend judgement or disbelief. I am always fascinated to see this in action as people change their thoughts and behaviours. In my work with The Hunger Project we are mindful not to patronise, limit or diminish anyone or anything within the village, irrespective of any difference in perspective. We achieve this because The Hunger Project *is* the village. Local people are charged as leaders. Change really is coming from within.

Evolution usually requires a shift in thinking. With any blind spot, it is particularly important to uncover and examine the beliefs that may be holding you back. Only then can you choose whether to keep the belief or not. A beautiful example of this comes from Malawi in the south eastern corner of Africa.

Malawi is a relatively small and exceptionally poor country, plagued by droughts and famines. In a rural workshop, local people were learning about HIV/AIDS, and examining some of the behaviours and practices that were causing it to spread. They were willing to examine how AIDS was spread, and determined to change any practice that might contribute to its growth. They did not want themselves or their children to continue to die from the disease.

In this village, people discussed a particular belief they had about young girls. According to a village superstition, it was thought that when a girl reached puberty, she started to produce 'oil' that could lead to infertility and that this 'oil' needed to be removed so she would be able bear a child.

To remove the 'oil' and prevent the young girl from being barren, the elders would bring a man to her to engage in sexual intercourse. The practice served an additional purpose of inducting the girl into womanhood at the onset of her menstruation. The strength of this belief in these 'oils' meant that both women and men in the village supported the practice.

It was essential for the community to discuss the 'oil' ritual in the context of practising safe sex, along with valuing and protecting girls. During the workshop, they learnt that that their belief about removing 'oils' through intercourse was erroneous, so after much discussion the community unanimously agreed to stop the practice. Through education, they now understood that there was no actual oil and that a girl's fertility was not determined this way.

However, the older women still wanted some way of marking the girls' transition to womanhood, so they created a new custom to celebrate this. They did this by sequestering the girls with older women to learn the ways of womanhood.

There is much about the old custom that is anathema to our western sensibilities, but finger wagging never helps. Indeed, recent generations used to believe equally spurious assumptions about 'vapours' and 'hysteria' for women. What I like about this story is that people surrendered an old belief for a new practice, and they did it consciously and deliberately. They were determined to stop practices that spread HIV and nothing was off the table. They also refrained from 'throwing out the baby with the bathwater'. By transforming rather than abandoning a local ritual, they created valuable rites of passage for young women.

Things to think about: CHANGE

❧ Are you stuck in old ways of doing things that have now become an unhelpful habit? Perhaps you can genuinely look at what belief may be fuelling an unwanted behaviour, and think about what you can do to change it.

❧ Be bold and be willing to examine everything. With courage you can choose a new behaviour that is more reflective of the type of person you want to become.

GOATS AND LEVERAGE

In Africa, agriculture is one of the most important industries and so veterinarians are on the government payroll. Increased crop yields, increased capacity for farming and healthy livestock are critical to the survival of its people.

An important role a government vet performs is to immunise livestock. In some communities, this is predominantly cattle while in others, it is goats. Vets who work for the government have quotas for immunising livestock and the government expects these to be met. The importance of this work cannot be overstated. For many rural people, their goat or cattle herds are their entire livelihood. It can be the total sum of all their assets. If animals get sick and die prematurely, it can be disastrous for a family, and for the entire community.

Although important, it is a rare occurrence for all animals in a region to be successfully immunised. Why is this so? Despite their best intentions to fulfil their quotas, vets often struggle to be effective. In many cases, the animals are under the care of families who live in remote rural areas, away from towns. In order for a vet to immunise livestock, they have to chase the goats around trees and under bushes to get them jabbed. It's very hard to make your quota when you are forced to travel long distances just to find the animals; even before attempting to vaccinate them.

The root of this problem is linked to traditional ways of life. However, the solution proves to be a classic case of how strategically working in partnership solves problems. Before The Hunger Project Epicentre process was established in an area, people lived separate, isolated lives. Each person only had their individual voice, which no one else listened to. With the advent of the Epicentre, clusters of villages now come together to solve problems collectively. Their combined voices have power. They can demand resources and government programmes that were previously unattainable.

Their collective voices achieved results. In order to get the livestock properly immunised, the leaders of the Epicentre set aside a particular day. Everyone is notified when the vet is coming to the Epicentre. Herders from miles around then bring in their goats. The vet knows this and turns up with assistants to help. They still spend all day immunising, but instead of wasting valuable time chasing animals, they now dispense the vaccines swiftly and efficiently. I've seen two thousand or so goats herded together for this process. The jabs are given, the goats are protected from disease, and the quotas are met.

Things to think about: LEVERAGE

- ❧ This deceptively simple example of leverage is accomplished organisationally through collaboration and partnership. If you have a think about your own business, in what aspect are you 'chasing goats'? This is also known as 'working *in* your business rather than *on* it'.

- ❧ A partnership can have a number of different agendas, but will be mutually beneficial. Who can help you succeed, and by doing so ensure their needs are also met?

- ❧ Ask yourself what actions you are taking now that are akin to chasing goats. If you take a step back, what can you focus on, bringing others together for a shared outcome? This way, everyone achieves their purpose together.

Creating a Supportive Environment

L eadership rarely occurs in a vacuum. The environment we live in – be it work, family or community – is the context from which we draw power. Our environment can either support or hinder us. Yes, our own decisions and actions are important; however, a crucial influence is the social, legal, political and financial structures that support and shape our efforts to sustain change.

Creating a supportive environment is the sixth step in the Nine Steps of Transformative Leadership framework. The characteristics that make an environment a supportive or enabling one are the attitudes, policies and practices that facilitate people's ability to take action. It can be as simple as having laws that actually work. In India for example, the 2009 Right to Education Act mandates compulsory education for young girls. This Act provides women with the enabling environment necessary for them to take a stand and demand their daughters receive an education.

In a supportive environment, people are aware of their rights (to education, the justice system, etc); can access it (without discrimination); can afford it (subsidised or free education, healthcare) and have a say in the running of those systems (elections, open press, freedom of speech). This process is as true for individuals as it is for societies, and is fundamental to what each of us need in order to thrive.

Family and work environments can be supportive when there is good communication, respect, accountability and encouragement to grow and evolve. We all recognise when we are not in an enabling environment. Paying attention to the emotional, physical and social structures that support us is vital.

Understanding the concept of an enabling and supportive environment can be transformative. It dispels the myth that the issue or set of issues we are facing is our personal failure and we are to blame. It sets personal struggle in an environmental context.

It's not the fault of those experiencing hunger that they are hungry. It's not the fault of the daily wage earner who labours sixteen hours a day that he still doesn't make enough to feed his family. It's not the fault of the fifteen-year-old girl that she is married and not able to attend school. Working alone or with a few others may not be sufficient to shift the system that gives rise to the structures causing hunger. Acknowledging this and transforming this context is why this step of creating a supportive and enabling environment is key to both personal and social change.

We all live in a society and at times we need help or support beyond our individual capacity. Supportive environments don't just happen. At a society level, active citizenry is an ongoing responsibility.

In this chapter, you will read how a community altered its relationship with 'the Spirit of Death', thus shedding light on the ways in which limiting beliefs can hold us back. This outcome was possible because of the environment, which paved the way for a powerful inquiry. You'll also see how the power of play created an environment where real social issues could be addressed and dealt with.

KAMALA – A PROBLEM SHARED

I visited India with some employees from a large Australian bank to meet and learn from local women leaders as part of a leadership programme with The Hunger Project. The Australian bankers were there to learn about leadership from the village women. For many of them, accepting the concept that they were the students rather than the masters was disorientating. (Often for us well-educated western-ers, our vanity makes us think that we are the smartest people in the room. As you can see from the stories in this book, this is usually not the case!)

On this particular day, there were about eight of us visiting a rural village where we met with a group of women in a small hut. Our aim was to interact and share life experiences – to talk about what life was like in our respective worlds; with all of our differences, similarities, sense of connection and our 'one-ness'. From a practical perspective, the bankers were there to try to understand the challenges the village women faced and what they were doing to overcome them. Our In-dian hosts were excited to host a meeting and to welcome us foreign-ers into their village. While it was out of the norm, it was a diversion they relished. There was a high level of curiosity on both sides.

The discussion commenced with just a handful of Indian women, but slowly, more and more women drifted in and soon there were about thirty of us present. We all sat on mats talking and connecting across a divide of language and circumstance.

The Australians first questioned the villagers. We wanted to know all about their lives. What they ate? How far they had to walk for water? What their various challenges were? I felt sure that their answers would focus on their immediate issues, which I knew were substan-tial. Some areas had little access to water, for example, and, for older people in particular, life was extremely hard. The women answered some of our questions; however, curiously, they did not want to fo-

81

cus on their challenges or hardships at all. What they did want to talk about was their achievements. They were extremely proud and were exceptionally clear about their vision for their community.

The Indian women had lots of questions for us, too. Because these women were mainly local government leaders at the village council level, the number one subject they were interested in was our electoral system. They wanted to know whether we had reserved seats or quotas for women politicians in our country. How many women were on our local councils? What were our political priorities?

One of the Australian bankers was a woman who held a senior role within her organisation. She ruefully answered, 'No, we don't have positions reserved for women in government, and, in fact, women are poorly represented both politically and in business, despite years of effort.' The Indian women were transfixed and sympathised with her at this state of affairs.

One of the village women leaders named Kamala reached across to the Australian woman and touched her. Kamala is an elected woman leader in her village, and her strength blazed forth from her features. She is also non-literate and a subsistence agricultural farmer. She put her rough, dry hand into the Australian woman's hand and squeezed it. She leaned forward and told her, 'We hear you. Keep strong. We will support you.' Essentially, she was telling the banker that she was on her team. She has it covered for us. She has our back!

For me, it was a very moving reminder of how we are all in this together. The Australian banker cried. She looked into Kamala's eyes and indeed at all the faces of the women leaders at the meeting. Their strength and solidarity, and their unifying purpose were deeply moving.

Things to think about: SUPPORT

❧ This story is a great reminder that others have trodden the path before us. There are signposts and guidance if we are willing to look for them. Our own liberation is tied up with the freedom and empowerment of others.

❧ It takes great humility to learn new things and contribute in a meaningful way. It can be difficult to do because it means making ourselves vulnerable, and many of us may not be used to being humble.

❧ Think about your own work environment. Are there other people around you who you just assume don't have anything you can learn from? What would happen if you reached out to them? You might be surprised!

THE SHEEP AND THE LION

Learning through playing games is a wonderful way to share experiences. Fun is not encouraged enough in our work and our lives. One of the games Indian women play in leadership training programs is called 'Goat and Tiger' or 'Sheep and Lion', depending on which part of the country you are in.

I'll explain the rules of the game here and leave you to figure out my reasons for telling you about it. I've introduced the game into corporate workshops, and it can get pretty feisty. In the training sessions in India, a lot of rough and tumble goes along with it. Although it's fun, people play to win!

In Indian villages, the players are women leaders who are voted into local council. Many are non-literate and from the lower castes. The women are used to having little influence in the broader affairs and decision-making within their village. The purpose of the game is to awaken them to their rights and encourage them to become real leaders.

Typically, about thirty women are involved in playing the game. They are asked to choose a couple of 'sheep' from their group. Of the remaining participants, one or two women volunteer to be the 'lion'. The sheep have to be protected from the lion. To do this, the remaining women hold hands and form a circle to create the 'fence'. The sheep are inside the circle. The lions are outside the 'fence'.

The game is played two or three times, with recalibration and discussion after each scenario. The game begins with the lions trying to get inside the fence to eat the sheep. The fence (the women holding hands) has to work hard to keep the lion out. The women have to stick together and not allow the lion to get inside the circle. If the lion catches the sheep, the game ends.

In the first run through of the game, the lions often find a break in the fence and grab the 'delicious' sheep quite easily. The women (fence) are not working together at this stage. There are gaps.

All that is needed is one weak link and the lion is able to force her way through to get to the sheep.

When the game is played a second time, the fence is much more rigorous. So the lion might attempt to strike a bargain to try to convince the fence to let it through. The fence usually withstands the lion's different approaches at either using brute force to crash through, or wheedling to make an arrangement. There is a lot of shrieking, pushing and laughing.

In the final game, it is rare for the lion to get through the fence. The women who are acting as the fence talk briefly before the game starts. They are aligned with a common goal. They are tight. The lion will go hungry in this round!

After the third game, the women gather and sit back on the meeting room floor. The trainer first asks each woman who played the sheep what it was like to be a sheep. Their answers are usually a variation of, 'Initially I felt frightened and powerless, but with the protective fence (the other women) we thought we would be okay'. Then the lions are asked about what it was like to be a lion. 'It was easier at first when the fence did not understand the danger or was not organised, but with each game it became harder.'

Finally, the women who acted as the fence are asked about what it was like to be a fence. They share: 'It was difficult at first. We had no plan or strategy. The lion was so strong and just pushed through the fence, but eventually we stood firm. We realised we had strength in working together'. The women sometimes mention that the lion offered inducements to try to get the sheep, and they discuss whether this deal was tempting or not.

An in-depth conversation then occurs where the trainer asks the women to identify the sheep in their village. They might answer that the sheep are the widows, the children or the disabled. They are the members of their community who are vulnerable to hunger, neglect or abuse. When asked to identify who the fence is, women see them-selves as fences. It is they who are charged to protect the needy and vulnerable. 'Who are the lions?' asks the trainer. Women are quick to answer. 'The shopkeeper who weights the scales, so people don't get all the rice they pay for,' answers one. 'Drunk and violent men,' answers another. Everyone nods and agrees with these responses.

The trainer then asks, 'When are you being the lion?' The women are quiet. Then one answers, 'I'm a lion when I'm unkind to my daughter-in-law.' Another says, 'I am a lion when I try to take food that is not mine.' It's always an amazing conversation. Here are women from deprived, rural India, who are being trained as leaders, asking themselves not only how they are victims of the system, but how they can be part of the problem.

Some of the other key principles that the women uncover through playing this game include understanding how even the fence, which is meant to protect the weak, sometimes colludes with the powerful. They see that if the sheep (the weak) strategise and unite, they can protect themselves from the lions in society.

Village women leaders learn that they need to build support in the village and the wider community to be able to protect themselves from the lions in the system. The lions are on the lookout to catch the women out and undermine their agenda for change.

Things to think about: PLAY

- The depth of the messages conveyed by this simple game always takes my breath away when I observe it. I've now seen this game in action a few times, and I'm repeatedly reminded how important it is to apply a similar thought process to my own life.

- It's worth asking: 'When am I being the lion? And when am I being the sheep?' Can I be a better 'fence' – a strong support to protect the vulnerable? If there is no fence, will you work to create one?

- ❧ These simple games are incredibly insightful when looking at the power of play. Leaders learn that they too need support as they lead – or manage – in order to create better awareness amongst everyone in the team.

BLIND SPOTS AND THE SPIRIT OF DEATH

One of the by-products of belonging to any culture, including adherence to its particular cultural norms, is that we also tend to inherit its blind spots. Every society has them. They are in part defined by the way we think and what we believe. A cultural blind spot includes unexamined assumptions or beliefs we automatically take for granted about the way things are. By nature, blind spots are easier to spot in cultures other than our own. Some are trivial; others rob us of our ability to authentically choose how we live our life. Often we think we are choosing, but mostly we inherit and repeat patterns of behaviour, end up somewhere and wonder how it happened. As Joseph Campbell so aptly points out, '… we spend our life climbing to the top of the ladder, only to find out it was up against the wrong wall.' One blind spot shared by most, if not all, western societies is that money and status will make us happy. So we work hard to make money in order to consume more to validate ourselves, hoping we will feel better. It is 'the truth' for so many of us that to challenge this or step outside is truly to feel like a fish out of water.

In this story, we see how an African community was able to overcome its own cultural blind spot regarding HIV/AIDs. For nearly twenty years, this disease had decimated previously healthy, adult populations of Africa. People were dying in their most productive years, leaving behind schools without teachers, hospitals without nurses and children without parents.

People sometimes forget that HIV is a preventable disease. Its spread is driven by a host of behaviours which, in turn, are driven by values, beliefs and mindsets held within society.

In a remote rural village in the small East African country of Malawi, an HIV/AIDS workshop run by The Hunger Project is being held under a big tree. Most of the one hundred people attending are non-literate subsistence farmers. They eat what they grow and, if the crops fail, they go hungry. AIDS is a huge problem in the community; one they are determined to find answers for in the course of this workshop.

The workshop – run by trained local volunteers called *animators* – is divided into three parts. Firstly, the facts about HIV and how it is spread are taught. Secondly, it addresses the root causes of the spread of AIDS, including the endemic gender roles, whereby many men define themselves through their sexual prowess and the number of lovers they have, and women all too often are unable to determine where, when, how and with whom sex takes place. Thirdly, the community comes up with strategies to change behaviours and practices so that AIDS is eradicated in the village.

This particular workshop is going well. People have grappled with many issues, and there is broad agreement that action must be taken to halt the spread of HIV/AIDS. The Malawian workshop facilitator is pleased, as well he should be. Having an authentic conversation about sex and AIDS can be fraught; akin to being in outback Australia in the 1930s, discussing sex and being shown how to use condoms.

Toward the end of this session, a tribal elder stands up and says that he understands now how the virus is spread, and he wants to ensure that all possible action occurs to rid his village of HIV. 'However,' he says, 'you do not understand about our village. We need to appease our ancestors so as not to unleash the *Spirit of Death*.'

As it turns out, appeasing ancestors is antithetical to safe sex practice. The people who lived in this area believed that, whenever a man died, the ancestors needed to be appeased with a particular cleansing ritual. Within three days of a man's death, so as to acknowledge the ancestors, the elders brought another man from the village to the widow for her to have sex with. If she did not do this, then the *Spirit of Death* would be unleashed and kill a member of her family. This would happen each week until the spirit was appeased. And the *Spirit of Death* did not like condoms.

Now, regardless of any opinion or judgement about whether the woman would want to have sex with some random man within three days of her husband's death, this practice was clearly at odds with trying to prevent AIDS. The husband may have died of AIDS and infected his wife, who could now pass it on to the other man. Or the new man might be infected and could infect the widow, who could then possibly get pregnant and give birth to an HIV-positive baby.

In response to these concerns about appeasing the *Spirit of Death*, an extraordinary conversation in the workshop ensues. The Malawian trainer listens to the villagers and does not agree or disagree with them. He certainly does not dismiss their belief as backward or nonsense. He poses a number of questions to them.

The trainer asks the locals if the villagers about twenty kilometres away hold the same beliefs. Do they too have an ancestral spirit that killed their people? People think about that and say, 'No'. He then asks, 'Why not?' The community give this some thought and cannot come up with a satisfactory answer. They share that 'Surely God does not love us any less than the people down the road.'

The trainer then introduces them to the idea of 'framing' and how beliefs come into being. He suggests that perhaps people many years ago had made up this belief for an extremely compelling reason, but now it wasn't beneficial and so could be rethought. Was it actually true? Would the *Spirit of Death* truly be unleashed this way? Was there really a *Spirit of Death*? These are powerful questions. The community is asked to consider that if someone made it up, then people have the power to do one of three things. They could keep the belief, stop it or change it. Everyone participates in the discussion that shines light and consciousness on a belief that is killing them.

The trainer then asks everybody what they want to do. The group breaks off so they can meet and discuss the issue. Everyone comes back after a period of time. The tribal elder stands again to announce the villagers' stance regarding the problem. He tells the trainer that even though they know the practice is responsible for spreading the HIV virus, they still want to appease the spirit of their ancestors.

The trainer's heart sinks. 'Oh well, the people have made a decision,' he thinks.

However, there is a twist. The tribal elder continues, 'Even though the ancestors must be appeased, we're not stupid. We don't want to die!'

In their discussions, they had come up with a change to the practice that was innovative and remarkable. And it went like this: When a man dies, within three days, the widow will invite a married member of her family or extended family to come to her hut. This married relative and their husband or wife would then have sex on the same mat where the widow and her (now deceased) husband used to make love. Afterwards, the widow would make a hot dish – usually something simple like heated maize – and give it to her female relative to eat. While eating, the relative would offer her act up to the ancestor's spirit, saying that she and her husband had done this as a proxy on behalf of the widow.

How would the people know the ancestors had accepted this ritual? Through sweating! When the woman sweated, this would let the ancestors know that the cleansing ritual had been accepted. What I love about this solution is its foolproof nature. Sweating is absolutely guaranteed. Malawi has a hot climate. The couple is inside an enclosed hut, which is hot. They've just had aerobic exercise and, if all that fails, they have something hot to eat – sweating will definitely occur!

This new practice has quickly become the norm in this small African village. My Malawian colleague who relayed the story said he could have sat in his office in Blantyre for twenty years and still not come up with such a brilliant solution to the problem!

Surely there are resonances for all of us when sifting through our own blind spots. This story emphasises not just how our limiting beliefs, which might seem quite reasonable to us, may actually be holding us back – but also, how these beliefs can be transformed.

When I think about this story, I am struck by how the villagers found a way to honour the past and move on with the future that they were committed to – one free from HIV/AIDS. They demonstrate a willingness to give up or alter comfortable traditions for a new possibility and a fresh chance at life. It always takes courage and risk to give something up like the old *Spirit of Death* custom. Through extraordinary ingenuity and creativity, the villagers crafted a life-affirming solution.

I learned much also from the animator trainer who led the workshop. He rightly believed that the people were capable of understanding the issues and making the decisions that were good for their community. He allowed the villagers to come up with their own solutions. He was willing to allow them to make the decision not to change. He did not judge them or their beliefs. He did not manipulate the situation for a particular outcome. Rather, he respected their process and made sure they had the necessary facts and the space to enable them to choose. Because of this, they were free to find a creative solution.

Things to think about: BLIND SPOTS

❖ I often refer to this story in my leadership development workshops. It's a powerful one. What is your own *Spirit of Death* belief? We all have one. How is it killing off new possibilities for your future? Take the time to identify yours. If you can't find this yourself, ask someone who knows you well. They might see something you can't, because often these beliefs are hidden in our blind spots. And they are there, trust me!

❧ Your own *Spirit of Death* might be a belief that you need to do everything yourself because people can't be trusted. Is it that more and more money will make you happy? Take the time to think about it and see what emerges.

❧ Consider what might now be possible for your own life when you let go of limiting ideas and behaviours.

MARY AND GENEVA – TWO SIDES OF THE SAME COIN

Sometimes it just seems that a bad situation can't be helped. It's either too hard to make a difference, or simply impossible. But is this actually true?

One time, while I was in Uganda, I visited a village near Kirahura in the southwest of the country. I was meeting some of the people who live within ten kilometres of The Hunger Project Epicentre. As I've mentioned elsewhere, an epicentre is the community mobilisation centre, built by the local people themselves. The epicentre runs training sessions, a health clinic, demonstration farms, a food bank and a microfinance bank. It can support the activities of around ten thousand people.

While walking through one of the villages and stopping at random huts to speak with the people living there, I met Geneva. Geneva was a widow with four children. She seemed to be in her mid-thirties. She met me wearing a yellow T-shirt. It was filthy, as many clothes are when soap is a luxury item.

Geneva's house was a two-room mud building. The cooking was done inside and the lingering smell of smoke in the house was strong. Her one bed was sectioned off with a piece of fabric tacked on to the ceiling. Geneva shared the single mattress with two of her children. To support herself and her family, she found sporadic work as a field hand. When I met her there wasn't much work available as it was just before the harvest.

None of Geneva's children attended school because, even though education was free, she could not afford to pay for school uniforms and books. Times were tough, and Geneva was understandably stressed and worried about her inability to care for her family. The future looked hopeless. She couldn't see any way out, and in talking to her, neither could I. I felt increasingly upset. It's just not fair. How can

94

people get ahead when there is so little opportunity? I felt helpless in the face of her circumstances.

After talking to Geneva, I wandered down a dirt path, winding my way through a banana plantation. I came across a similar two-room home made of mud which was owned by a woman called Mary. Curiously, Mary was also wearing a yellow T-shirt and she too was a widow with four children to care for, two of whom were the children of her recently deceased daughter. Mary also worked as a field hand when work was available.

The similarities ended there. Mary's whole being radiated joy and hope even though her material situation was virtually the same as Geneva's. I was deeply curious about this. How was this possible? What was the impetus for her positivity?

It turns out that about a year ago, Mary had received training through the Vision, Commitment and Action Workshop – part of The Hunger Project's program to unlock the mindset and leadership of local people to combat hunger. In practical terms, Mary shared that she now thought differently about every aspect of her life. For instance, whereas a year ago her children didn't go to school because of the cost, these days their education was at the top of her priorities. Mary said, 'Every bit of money I get, I think how much can I put into my children's schooling.' As a result of her training in agriculture at the local epicentre, Mary was growing different plants in her kitchen garden, which gave her nutritional options beyond bananas and maize. She had borrowed some money from the microfinance bank and used it to buy a goat, which was munching on the grass next to her hut. Mary had plans for the future; in fact she said she now felt very positive about the future.

In her whole being, Mary offered a direct contrast to Geneva. After speaking to Mary, I felt encouraged. I was reminded again of the power of the human spirit. Each and every person has the capacity to turn their situation around. We don't need handouts, or someone to do it for us. Such a solution is rarely long-term and does nothing to develop someone's innate abilities and resourcefulness. Nevertheless, we often can't do it on our own. We need support.

The difference between Mary and Geneva highlights how crucial the enabling environment is. For Mary, this meant the ability to access the epicentre programs and the support structure associated with it. In contrast, Geneva hadn't been able to create the same positive outcomes in her life. There is nothing inherently hopeless about Geneva – put you or me in her situation and, no doubt, we would feel the same way. Being connected to the epicentre influenced Mary's mindset and attitudes which, in turn, led to corresponding behaviours. As a result, Mary now believed that she could feed her family, and while her situation had not fully turned around, she was clearly on track. All of her children looked healthy and were clean. This is not simply positive thinking. Just wishing for something doesn't make it happen. Even entrenched behaviours or beliefs can be changed, but they need corresponding actions to deliver results.

For me, meeting these two women was a powerful lesson in the resilience and capability of human beings. I felt so disheartened after meeting Geneva that I too felt resigned. In that moment, I honestly believed that her situation couldn't improve. I agreed with her that it all seemed hopeless, and I even wondered how I might surreptitiously leave some money behind. Not as a gesture toward her new life, but in admitting nothing else was possible for Geneva and her family but more misery and hopelessness.

Mary resembled Geneva one year ago. Prior to her training in the Vision, Commitment and Action Workshop, she had also felt despondent and lacked hope and impetus. She didn't educate her kids or see any joy in the future.

Before I left Mary and Geneva's village, I introduced Geneva to the local trained volunteer leader, who promised to invite her to upcoming workshops on nutrition, income and other things. I'm confident that when Geneva connects with the epicentre activities, she will find support and motivation to help unlock her ability to embrace a brighter future.

Things to think about: SUPPORTIVE ENVIRONMENTS

❧ Meeting Mary and Geneva reminds me that even the most desperate situations can be transformed. Regardless of where you're at, things can change!

❧ What support is available to you? Who can help you through a tough spot?

❧ Understanding the power of the enabling environment can lessen the sense of failure we often have when we struggle and fall. It makes the situation less personal. That said, we can strive to create environments that support us. Do an audit of what's not supporting you in your life. Friends that keep you small, or unsafe or toxic work environments that leave you stressed and unfulfilled are examples of disabling environments that you can take action to change.

❧ Challenge your thinking by seeking outside input. If you're struggling, it can be hard to see the assistance that's readily available. You may need to broaden your search to outside your immediate circles.

Finding New Ways

The road to success is never a straight one. It is littered with deviations and obstacles. Ongoing calibrations are always needed to keep you on course. When you set out to achieve something remarkable, obstacles will invariably get in the way.

Stuff happens and things don't always go as expected. Sometimes when things don't go the way we hoped, we become demoralised. We might start to question our purpose, our activity or our commitment; all of which undermines our optimism and enthusiasm for the task at hand. We are adept at responding to circumstances: to feel good when things are going our way and to feel bad when they don't. It's not personal, but it feels as though it is. Too many of us give up when we come up against criticism, setbacks or perceived failures.

Developing resilience and finding new approaches to conquering problems and setbacks are key: these traits comprise the seventh step in the Nine Steps of Transformative Leadership process. You need to be willing to ask yourself the question: when things are not going to plan, who am I going to *be*? Rather than let the circumstances dictate your response, you can tap into internal resilience, focus, and find another way. In fact, in my experience, whenever I experience setbacks, I lean into them. It can often be a sign I'm onto something! I may need to change an approach or find another way, but I resolve to keep going.

Sometimes when we hear about people who have become famous through their stellar achievements, we can feel dispirited. We may feel that our shortcomings are the result of us not being good enough. But when we hear of someone's challenges – their 'long dark night of the soul' – and the fact that they failed miserably before their 'overnight' success, they become human. Or as Thomas Edison was reported to have once said, 'I have not failed. I've just found 10,000 ways that didn't work'

In this chapter, you'll meet people who overcame incredible odds to achieve their goals. Saroj was ridiculed and faced a huge backlash, but she seized every opportunity to help her community. Amri Bhai was resilient and persistent in the face of withering criticism. She pushed through to deliver tangible and remarkable outcomes.

Both of these women refused to stop at 'No'. They inspire us to keep going, even when nothing looks certain. They tapped into the strength of their vision, their own leadership and the power of their community to continue along their path and succeed.

AMRI BHAI – ACCEPTING FEEDBACK

Amri Bhai lives in a village about one hundred kilometres from Udaipur in the Indian state of Rajasthan. Conditions in this part of India are extremely harsh, and life is hard. Water is scarce; crops are marginal and the ground is rocky and dry. Child malnutrition is high, and literacy levels are significantly lower than in other parts of the country.

Amri Bhai is an enormously persistent woman. She sits on the local government council. She has a burning vision for her community that is unwavering. She is in a position to make positive changes within her village. But as a non-literate woman, she doesn't have direct social authority to be listened to and respected by others in power.

One thing most people, including the poorest members of Indian society, are unaware of is that the Indian government provides pensions for the most vulnerable. For instance, widows and old people are entitled to receive a pension. There are few things sadder than seeing an extremely old woman or man trying to carry heavy firewood or struggling with other manual labour in order to make a few rupees so they may eat. At a time when they should be able to put their feet up, they must continue to perform backbreaking work or otherwise face starvation. However, just because there is a government service available, does not mean that those people entitled to it know about it or can access it, especially when it necessitates filling out forms.

Through her training with The Hunger Project, Amri learned that old people and widows were entitled to a government pension. This was surprising news to her. Neither she nor her community knew it was available. In Amri's village there were about a dozen widows and old people for whom survival was a constant challenge due to lack of food and housing.

Amri Bhai made it her priority to find out about how to access these pensions. She collected the names of all the eligible people and then caught a bus to the closest government office. It was nearly a day's travel to get to and from the town, but she was determined to get these people's names registered for the pension. She met with the local bureaucrat, who ignored her. On more than twenty occasions, Amri caught the bus into town to meet with the relevant government officer to get her people on the pension, and each time he refused to help her. Eventually, the bureaucrat witheringly asked her, 'Why should I do anything for you? You can't even read or write.'

Now there are many ways Amri could have responded to this rude dismissal. After all, she was an elected leader! How dare he speak to her like that!

Amri's response is a lesson in taking on the feedback and getting on with things. She knew that complaining and feeling like a victim as a result of his disrespectful treatment of her wouldn't help those people relying on her to get their pensions. So Amri went back to her village. She enrolled in a literacy course, and practised writing by scraping letters onto rocks. Yes, you read that correctly. Amri couldn't afford paper and pencil, but that didn't stop her. She learned to write using sharp stones as a pen and larger rocks as paper.

It took her three months, but she eventually learned enough to fill in the dozen government forms in her own handwriting. It was very rudimentary, but it was writing. She returned to the government office to present the forms to the bureaucrat, who was shocked! He had no choice but to stamp the forms and put the names in the system. Soon these impoverished people were receiving small monthly payments that allowed them to survive. I met a number of them when I visited her village a while later. One very old woman stood in a meeting and spoke very emotionally. She kept touching her stomach and her shoulder, all the while pointing at Amri. What she was saying was 'I now have food because of her. I was so hungry. I had nothing.

I didn't even have anything to wear, and now I have this sari.' It was very moving to witness this outpouring of gratitude from this very old and frail woman.

Like many leaders, Amri Bhai epitomises persistence and resilience. Amri focused on an outcome and did not allow herself to become derailed by any obstacles on her path. She was less concerned with what people thought of her and more focused on the result. She took the feedback on board and responded to it, even though the feedback was meant to belittle and intimidate her. Amri was able to hear the message and took it upon herself to become literate. She understood that for her to make the biggest difference she would need extra skills, and she set about mastering them. Above all else, she was persistent. She kept showing up!

Things to think about: ACCEPTING FEEDBACK

- How often do we give up when we hear negative feedback, especially from someone in authority?

- Often we settle for our limitations; listing our shortcomings as the reason as though they were fixed in stone. Like Amri, we should identify them and then take the necessary actions to overcome them.

- In Amri's case, it was her writing that was her shortcoming. What's yours? Could you take something new on in order to up skill yourself and prove you're capable?

SAROJ – DOING THE RIGHT THING

How often do we hold back from achieving something because we worry about what other people might think? Recently, I met Saroj – a diminutive and extremely determined woman from a rural village in Rajasthan, India. This area is terribly dry and rocky, and the whole state commonly suffers from a great deal of hunger and poverty. Accessing clean water in Saroj's village is a huge issue, and there is limited education and an entrenched distrust around educating girls.

After hearing about the upcoming council elections, Saroj decided to stand for one of the village councillor positions. This was a bold move as she had been previously abandoned by her husband, which made her life additionally difficult in her small, traditional village. Nevertheless, Saroj won a seat on the council and became an elected woman leader.

Once elected, Saroj attended the Women's Leaders Workshop run by The Hunger Project. Like other women before her, she was excited by the opportunity this role afforded her to help the poor and vulnerable in her community. Even though some people in the village had a negative attitude towards her, Saroj was undeterred by their disapproving opinions. She attended council meetings to implement positive change within her village as an elected woman leader.

Saroj discovered that a number of wealthier families were receiving government food aid that was allocated for the poorest families. This food aid consisted of small rations of rice, lentils and oil – just enough to keep families alive. She decided that her first priority should be to clean up these lists and so she took a stand to combat this injustice. She was sick of poor and vulnerable families literally wasting away because they were being unfairly denied the most basic of provisions. Saroj approached the families who were abusing the system, informing them that they were to be removed from the government food lists.

Her actions resulted in an immediate backlash. Saroj was scorned, intimidated and threatened. However, she remained undeterred and held firm in order to ensure that the poorest families were added to the government list for food assistance. This change enabled these families to survive during the non-harvesting months.

Saroj then set about correcting negative attitudes towards education within her village. Even though she had no literacy skills, Saroj understood the opportunities an education offered children in this rural community. A number of families weren't sending their children to school (which is free and provided by the government), either because of their beliefs against educating their daughters, or because children were needed to earn money by working in the field. Saroj visited these families as many as twenty-five times until eventually all of them placed their children into school. Her remarkable persistence paid off, and when I met her, every single eligible child had an outstanding school attendance record.

After the effects of Saroj's hard work were witnessed by the villagers, she was considered a champion and became accepted by the community. Saroj's most recent accomplishment was a truly monumental one. She learned that, thirty years earlier, the government had requisitioned a dam to be built in her drought-prone village where water was a scarce resource. However, within that time, nothing had happened. Saroj lobbied the government so successfully that construction on the dam started immediately. Once completed, it provided safe drinking water and irrigation for many nearby villages.

Saroj is one of those women who are a force of nature. Her physical stature belies her gigantic spirit. She did not allow the naysayers to stop her. Nor did she give up when she saw the right thing to do, even though it made her unpopular and a possible target for reprisal. Saroj demonstrates incredible courage and focus. She saw that something needed to be done in her village, and she seized the opportunity to do so.

Saroj stepped up to the challenge of making a difference. She put up with intimidation and threats while she went about righting wrongs and giving a voice to the poor. Saroj accomplished work so transparently, whether it was finding a way for children to attend school or getting a dam built, that people eventually viewed life through her perspective. She did not stop at the first snide comment or round of verbal abuse. Nor did she give up when the going got tough.

Things to think about: DOING THE RIGHT THING

❧ Too often we let people's opinion determine our actions. Either we don't want to upset the system, or we fear being unpopular. In Australia the 'tall poppy syndrome' can keep us living in a mediocre way because we live in fear of someone's ridicule. But, in the end, what is more important? Living a life that truly mattered, where you made a difference and were true to your dreams? Or keeping yourself small so as to not upset someone? Saroj was not willing to accept living a mediocre life, and hundreds of families were undeniably better off because of her actions.

❧ It's so common to hold back because we worry about what people think. Saroj demonstrates the power of courage and inspired single-mindedness.

❧ If you see something that needs to be done, and you hesitate, think about Saroj. Are there things in your life that you want to do, but haven't stepped forward because you're worried about other people's reactions? What might happen if you forged ahead and just did it?

THE UNREASONABLE PATH OF PROGRESS

I want to talk about being unreasonable and reclaim this word from its negative connotations. It is a word that can make us pause, then push through to the vein of gold. Throughout this book, I've remarked on how 'unreasonable' people have been, and I've said this with the utmost admiration and respect. Interestingly, in the first edit of this book, my editor urged me to find an alternative word for 'unreasonable' because of its negative associations. Couldn't I use 'brave', 'determined' or 'stoic' instead?

It puzzled me at first that anyone would hold the definition of 'unreasonable' predominantly in a negative light. Yet, I can understand it through the antonym of 'reasonable', which is regarded by many people as being a virtue. However, seeing unreasonable behaviour singularly as a flaw has limitations, especially when this type of behaviour is actually called for.

I choose to use the word as intended by George Bernard Shaw when he said, 'The reasonable man adapts himself to the world; the unreasonable one persists in trying to adapt the world to himself. Therefore, all progress depends on the unreasonable man.'

Throughout this book, and in my own life, I talk about and believe that ending world hunger is possible and doable. I'm also on the team that thinks it can be done by 2030! This is completely unreasonable! 'Are you mad?' people might ask. And I get it. Against the prevailing belief that hunger has always shadowed humanity and always will, the idea of actually ending it seems absurd. Even more unreasonable is the expectation that the people we normally perceive as being hopeless and helpless will be the leaders in this unprecedented human achievement! It's totally unreasonable to expect that a non-literate village woman could bring education to her village, or demand services to assist the vulnerable from middle-class bureaucrats who resent having to help her fill out forms. It's totally unreasonable to expect that men will give up their power in order to experience the power of partnership with women. It's totally unreasonable to expect that people in cosseted Western countries will confront their own consumption and spiritual wasteland, and join the movement to end hunger. And yet, all of this is happening despite it being unreasonable. Without unreasonableness, nothing of importance ever happens. Nothing!

Being unreasonable interrupts the status quo. It's not 'business as usual'. It kills complacency, and it offers hope. We come alive when we are part of a great, magnificent, unreasonable endeavour! That is why World War II veterans often relate to their wartime experiences as some of the best in their lives, despite suffering great loss, personal hardships and risks to their safety. It seems as though the act of taking part in something bigger than yourself – something that you believe in and where there are no guarantees – is life affirming. This is totally unreasonable!

Let's examine the track record of 'reasonableness' up against the task of achieving vital progress. In this context, reasonableness is not about functionality. In many countries, it's reasonable to assume people will drive on the correct side of the road. This is not what I am talking about when I talk about being unreasonable.

In a risk-averse culture, reasonableness easily displaces vision. Reasonableness persuades us not to act on our own dreams. I'm talking about how we can too easily settle for living a life devoid of personal quest, where the ultimate aim is to be comfortable. In this type of life, the goal seems to simply exist and try to avoid life's challenges until we die. Being reasonable does not bring change. At best, it perpetuates more of the same and, at worst, it can deaden us to possibility, vision and hope and leads to apathy. Being reasonable can be another way of never making a difference.

Notwithstanding humanity's need for reasonable behaviour to oil the wheels of social interaction, knowing our tendencies as human beings, I constantly challenge my own reasonableness. When I have an excuse about why something is or isn't possible, I check whether this is an excuse born of being reasonable. I do acknowledge that being unreasonable without reflection can manifest as sheer belligerence or 'pie-in-the-sky' delusions. I am not advocating unreasonableness as a justification for contrary behaviour. Nor is it a call to positive thinking masked as being unreasonable. For example, it would be unreasonable and delusional for me to declare that I'll run a marathon tomorrow. However, sometimes I'm aware that I'm just being too reasonable, which won't achieve the outcome I'm committed to. For me, a small (but important) example is all the excuses I make not to go to the gym: the rain; a pressing workload; or not having the right shoes with me. Once you have an ear for it, reasonableness soon sounds like evasion, procrastination or faint-heartedness.

Being 'unreasonable' in the fuller sense of the term occurs at the intersection of courage and vision. It takes courage to stand for something uncommon or deemed unlikely. Because it's so commonplace today, the fight that the suffragettes took on to secure the vote for women has become mainstream – and yet, at that time, they were perceived as totally unreasonable. They were ferociously courageous in support of their vision. They were laughed at, ridiculed and beaten. Of course, in most parts of the world, it's commonplace now for women to be able to vote. But back then, this viewpoint was a complete affront to the status quo.

Being unreasonable, like being courageous and being willing to push through to make something happen, exposes you to the risk of being unpopular. It's taking a stand for something unknown. The whole mechanism and weight of society's traditional values reacts against it. It should be viewed as a sacred charge in which you pick your battles. It is not for the faint-hearted.

A marginalised caste woman stopping child marriages is unreasonable. A family not accepting dowry is unreasonable. A man in a village speaking to other men about their duty to support their wives rather than beating them is unreasonable. Yet each of these acts breaks open the fabric of what's considered normal, and ushers in change for the better. What have you been reasonable about that you will now not tolerate? Steve Jobs of Apple once said, 'Let's hear it for the misfits!' Well I say, 'Let's hear it for the unreasonable!'

Things to think about: BEING REASONABLE

✤ How reasonable are you? What excuses do you commonly use that keep you in your bubble of normality where you accept things we profoundly wish to change?

✤ Can you take on a mantra of being unreasonable? What changes could you bring about in the world? What can you stand for that can only happen as a result of courage and vision?

✤ For many of us, even making changes that are inclusive, life honouring or just the right thing to do can seem all too hard. What stops you from making changes in your life and being willing to challenge the status quo?

✤ Being unreasonable requires bravery. It's about stepping outside your comfort zone to make some bold changes, and often that can be uncomfortable. Are you willing to feel uncomfortable in the way you usually do things in favour of finding new ways? How can you encourage others to be unreasonable?

Experiencing Success

After all the effort and toil, achieving your goal and finding success is richly rewarding. This is what it's all been for; where the hard work, setbacks and challenges give way to that sweet taste of victory.

What's interesting about success is that it isn't a destination. Once you achieve a certain goal, that's rarely the end. It is a punctuation point in a lifetime journey of growth and evolution. Success brings its own momentum – a small win can set you up to achieve bigger and better things. It is this practice that represents the eighth step in the Nine Steps of Transformative Leadership.

Success is subjective. We lose power around feeling successful when we compare ourselves with someone else. My success may not be your success. Success may involve founding a multi-million dollar company. Or it may be taking the risk to fall in love. Success may be installing a pit latrine with a tippy-tap hand washing system in your village in Zambia. Achieving this objective engenders real pride and satisfaction because you know your kids won't die from lack of sanitation. This achievement can then be the catalyst for the next improvement, and so success snowballs.

When success comes, it's important to acknowledge and celebrate it. Take the time to reflect and feel satisfaction. This helps cultivate a spirit of gratitude. After all, everything is relative. You can only be the best version of you. There is always more we can do. However, in practising gratitude, we can acknowledge what we've done to date, and draw inspiration and strength to take on the next big action.

In this chapter, we'll read about the village women who met with the director of a big foreign bank. Their measure of success is very different to his! Also we will meet Georgina, who created a mini empire in a remote village in Uganda, and Shanti, who selflessly set about helping others in her Indian village secure new housing before receiving a new home herself.

MEASURES OF WEALTH

On a bright, hot, sunny day, I walked with the managing director of one of Australia's largest investment banks through a rural area of Bangladesh. We were both passionate about the work of ending hunger and we were there to expand our skills as advocates by witnessing the situation first-hand. We met with a group of village women under a shady tree and started our discussion. Firstly, like any initial meeting anywhere in the world, we wanted to get to know each other. Chai tea was passed around and we settled in. The first question the village women asked us was, 'Are you married?' I showed them a photo of my husband and they oohed and aahed about how very handsome they thought he was. My banker friend explained he was married also.

The village women then inquired about our children. They looked at each other with pleasure as I told them I had a daughter and a son. They then asked if I lived with my mother-in-law (a situation common in South Asia). I explained that my husband, children and I lived in a separate home. They were amazed when I told them my husband was at home in Australia taking care of our children.

After our pleasantries, we got down to business. 'How many chickens do you have?' I was asked. I answered, 'Four'. They all liked that answer. My banker friend though, who lived in a big mansion in the city, didn't have any chickens. 'Hmmm' the women muttered, casting sorry glances at him.

Next we're asked, 'How many cows?' As I live on one hundred acres in the country, I was on firm ground here. 'Fifteen,' I remarked. The women then chattered and showed expressions of surprise. For me, the purpose for having cows is to keep the grass short. They are simply a means to an end. But for these women, clearly, I was a person of almost unimaginable wealth. The banker responded that he had none. 'Goats?' they asked. 'No', he replied. Amongst the village women, there was a mixture of sadness for him and delight in their comparative prosperity. This is the yardstick by which these women measure a person's wealth. So they, with their chickens and one cow, were doing all right compared to this poor foreign man.

The banker and I chuckled afterwards. These questions were the villagers' version of, 'What school did you go to?' and 'What do you do for a living?' It was these women's way of orienting where he and I were positioned in their world. And this is something that happens all over the world. I love the humanity of it!

Clearly, we all imbue relative wealth and status with different meanings and attachments. Many people in the world would see these women as 'poor'. And yet, these women felt sorry for our wealthy banker. In comparison to their livestock ownership, they felt rich. It's just a matter of perspective.

One of the things I often notice in my conversations with people around the world is how often we confuse wealth with having money. Someone is described as wealthy when they have lots of money, and yet, they can be the poorest in terms of their spirit, love and happiness. I now say that a person is 'financially wealthy' when I'm speaking about them in relation to their money. And I know many others whom I would see as living a life of great wealth, yet they don't have large financial resources.

By simply confining the word 'wealth' to a narrow parameter can, and often does, guide us towards things that may not be meaningful or satisfying. For me, true wealth is about being purposefully engaged in a meaningful life.

Things to think about: WEALTH

❧ It's really interesting to evaluate: what is wealth and how do you measure it? Is it having lots of money? Is it livestock? Is it having peace of mind, and a healthy, happy family? Is it how you compare yourself to others around you? Is it having the financial means to buy a new car or a bigger house? Is it something intangible?

❧ My perspective on wealth has fundamentally changed as a result of my work with The Hunger Project. I now believe wealth involves having a purpose in life and directing your energy into something truly meaningful.

GEORGINA – HARVESTING AN EMPIRE

While I was visiting Uganda, I met a truly entrepreneurial woman called Georgina. Her story is a real 'rags to riches' tale. Today, Georgina is a successful farmer, yet seven years ago she was living in a one-room mud hut with no sign of opportunity.

I heard about Georgina through conversations I'd had with some local women. I was keen to meet her because she was such an inspiration to her community. I drove through lush, green landscape and met Georgina at her home. It was set on about three acres of land, which she intensively cultivated. When I arrived, she was polite but brusque. Like many of us with a hectic schedule, Georgina made allowances given that we had stopped by to meet her. However, she clearly had other things to do. Georgina had a mini-empire to run, way out in the remote villages of Uganda, and she was a busy lady.

Efficiently, Georgina showed me around her property. She and her husband Paul first presented the four hundred chickens she owned for egg and meat production. They had built a large brick enclosure for them and there were birds everywhere.

Georgina then took me to the back of her property where she grew bananas. A sizeable plantation of mature plants yielded extremely impressive bunches of fruit. We walked together through the plantation where I saw people with machetes harvesting the crop.

However, by far her most profitable enterprise was pig farming. Georgina had more than fifty pigs and piglets. To run her farm business, Georgina hired eleven people from the village, so she was a significant income source for others. In addition to their business activities, Georgina and her husband (who were unable to have children themselves) adopted six children from local families who had lost their parents due to AIDS, and paid school fees for another twenty.

After seeing her businesses, I went inside to have some refreshments. Her house was a four-room brick and cement building with a tin roof. I sat on one of her two couches, covered with a crochet blanket. There were religious pictures, a photo of the president of Uganda and a lovely picture of her and her husband on the walls.

The more I learned about Georgina, the more intrigued I became to hear about her past. I wanted to know what had sparked the change within the last seven years of her life. She explained that she started out small and had grown from there. She'd borrowed money from The Hunger Project microfinance scheme and started with some chickens. As a result of her training as part of receiving the loan, she realised she could create a new life, and with the money she'd borrowed, she had the resources to begin. Her vision kept her moving forward; she was focused. She mostly ploughed the profits back into her enterprises and had only built her home two years before my visit. Her husband was an influential supporter of her success, and didn't accept comments made by men in the village that he should keep his wife under control. He was on her team and together they prioritised spending, and both undertook the arduous manual labour needed to start their new life.

As any entrepreneur reading this would know, success takes work and commitment. You start with a goal or a vision – even an idea. In Georgina's case, it was a tremendous one: that she and her husband would be free from hunger, and this freedom would be achieved through their own work and effort.

After drinking a cup of coffee together, I left Georgina. She had her businesses to take care of and could not stop to chat for long. Seven years ago, all of these achievements would have seemed unimaginable. Her next challenge was to find markets outside the surrounding villages. This would require better roads linking her village to nearby towns. She was visiting local government officials today to put pressure on them to actually develop and construct them. I'm sure she will be successful.

Things to think about: ENTREPRENEURIALISM

❧ To strike out and live the life we've dreamt of is much more possible than it was some years ago. We are lucky to have such opportunity and structures in place to 'walk to the beat of our own drum'. Georgina proves that true entrepreneurialism only needs the vision, and a desire to succeed regardless of what is thrown in front of you.

❧ Georgina's focus is the sort of focus that entrepreneurs need to succeed. Most entrepreneurs I know are obsessed workaholics following a crazy dream – and I say that with love and admiration! You have to be single-minded, as Georgina was, and seize opportunities. Where do you want to be in seven years' time? What will your world look like?

SHANTI – ROOM FOR ALL

Shanti is a non-literate woman leader from a village close to the Gujarat border in India. Conditions here are harsh. There is sparse rainfall for most of the year, and safe drinking water is difficult to find. When it does rain, homes are flooded, and children can get sick and die. The lack of adequate basic shelter exposes the vulnerable to disease. Most homes are made out of a mixture of sand and cow dung, with leaves and branches for roofs. These leak terribly during the short monsoon season, and walls crumble. Though brief, the monsoon takes its toll.

Shanti heard of a government program which allocated basic houses for the most marginal and vulnerable families already living on the *Below the Poverty Line* government subsidy. She set about accessing this programme on behalf of the poorest families in her village. The homes provided by the government are an extremely basic two-room dwelling, but they are made out of bricks and cement, and have a tin roof. They do not leak, and the walls do not crumble.

Through sheer tenacity and focused action, Shanti managed to assist five families to each gain access to one of these new houses. All of these families were itinerant farm workers, living below the poverty line. I met a number of them, and they were thrilled to be proudly showing off their new homes to me. I have a terrific photo of Shanti with a local woman, standing in the doorway of an unfinished new house. They both look so happy and proud.

Remarkably, Shanti and her own family still lived in a one-room mud hut, and for the six of them, it was a tight squeeze. When I sat with Shanti in her hut, I could not imagine how the family lived, cooked and slept within the walls of this structure. They suffered through the rainy periods and she'd nearly lost a child due to the poor living conditions. Shanti herself was also on the *Below the Poverty Line* list and, therefore was eligible for a new house. I asked her why she hadn't received one yet. Without hesitation, she told me she wouldn't apply to get a house until every other eligible family had one. This would take a few years.

Shanti is committed to leading by example. She had been elected to the local village council and, in a culture of corruption, to been seen as having ethical and impeccable behaviour was vitally important to her. She didn't want it said or intimated by others that she was using her elected role simply to gain the perks. She didn't want to jeopardise her vision for the difference she hoped to make. Shanti felt that if she were to receive one of the new houses before others on the *Below the Poverty Line* list it would undermine her ability to achieve her goals for her village.

She was selfless and strategic. Her vision for what she wanted to achieve was bigger than her personal situation.

Things to think about: LEADING BY EXAMPLE

- ❧ Shanti makes me think about how we can respond when we experience power. Are we out to 'feather our own nest', or are we more expansive and inclusive?

- ❧ Shanti was certainly successful, but her material world hadn't altered. However, she was full of pride, happiness and satisfaction.

- ❧ It's important to ensure you meet your own needs, but that doesn't mean doing nothing for others. How can we ensure each member of our family, team or world has what they need to flourish and succeed?

- ❧ What do you want to make happen that requires placing your own comfort on hold in order to realise your dream?

Giving Back

There are so many benefits to giving back. It is an act of leadership and generosity, and it allows us more room to grow. It is this crucial feat that represents the final step in the Nine Steps of Transformative Leadership.

When we give, we expand. It seems counter-intuitive, but in giving of ourselves, we aren't left with less. In giving our money, we realise how much we truly have. In helping others, something within us unfurls and grows. In contributing, we open the door for other positive things to happen in our life.

Through our actions, we are actively having a say about who we are and what we stand for.

Often people wait to give back. 'When I retire I'll have the time to mentor those kids', or 'When I make my millions, I'll donate to something that I believe in'. Some of us think we have to reach a certain point in our lives or reach some milestone in prosperity before we are in a position to give. Is it your threshold of personal comfort that inhibits you from giving?

Often we judge what we can give, and in finding ourselves wanting, we give nothing. We might feel that whatever we do give back is such a small drop in the ocean that it won't achieve anything. We don't think we have the money or time to give back, so why bother? And so, we routinely withhold from expressing generosity.

Within our culture, we experience an illusion of limited resources. We frequently feel we don't have enough, be it time, money, love … Hopefully, after reading this book you will become aware of the huge power we all have if we step up and contribute what we have, without judgment or assessment.

In this chapter, we'll see how whole-hearted giving is actually the antidote to feeling as though you don't have enough. We'll meet Kevin, a Hunger Project animator who understands what makes a person – or a world – secure and worthwhile to live in. And we'll meet some women farm workers whose generosity lives on for me through their special gift to me. Finally, we read how we all have special skills and talents that we can share to benefit others, as is the case with Rhada, who devoted her time and literacy skills to help educate others.

Giving back is a not about stroking one's ego or fulfilling a desire for recognition. It's an act of truth. It honours and recognises the opportunities we have been given in our lives. Giving back expresses gratitude for all that has been given to us.

THE BANGLE

While I was in Uttar Pradesh in India, I managed to hitch a ride on the back of a truck with some women farm workers. The women and I eyed each other off. I was a strange sight in this poor rural area. Not many white folk wandering around, and certainly not hitching rides to a remote farm area.

We were all squeezed in the back of an old truck. I couldn't speak their Hindi dialect, and they couldn't speak English. I didn't have an interpreter with me, but I could tell they were desperately and inventively trying to ask me something.

After a few attempts at communication, their questioning became clear – where was my jewellery? They searched my toes for a toe ring, my wrists for bangles and my neck for a necklace, my nose for a ring and my ears for earrings. Nothing! Their search was in vain since I wasn't wearing any.

The women looked at me with mixture of amazement and pity on their faces. One woman then slipped a battered silver-plated bangle from her own wrist and pushed my hand through it. Her face beamed, and all the women broke into laughter and clapped. This woman owned next to nothing, yet she still wanted to give me something. I now had a bangle, given to me by one of the poorest women on earth. I treasure this bangle and wear it often.

Things to think about: GIVING

❧ We all have a bit more than we think we do and we all have something we can give. What is your personal version of a bangle and a smile?

❧ When you see someone who doesn't have anything, do you give? How do you feel about giving money to someone on the street? In the case of this story, I was the person who lacked something. The woman on the truck made me feel wonderful with her gift. Besides sharing her wealth, she shared her Self.

❧ Being generous about sharing yourself with others is the greatest gift of all. Are you giving of yourself?

RHADA – THE GIFT OF LITERACY

I met Rhada in her small village in Bangladesh on a steamy afternoon. She was a trained volunteer leader for The Hunger Project. She was passionate about ending hunger and proved her commitment by running a female adult literacy class from 3.00 pm onwards for one and a half hours, six days a week.

Literacy rates for women, especially older women, were less than fifty per cent in Rhada's village. I was fortunate enough to observe one of her classes. It was held in a small tin shed with about twenty-five women crammed into the space. The women were full of excitement as they learned how to read and count numbers.

One woman emotionally shared her thoughts with me, 'I never knew how much pleasure reading and writing would give me. I can now read, but even if I only knew one word, this would mean everything to me.'

Rhada is passionate about education as a right for all. 'These women are never going to go to school or to university, but this doesn't mean they shouldn't know the joy and dignity of being able to write their own name, and understand the written word,' she said to me.

I asked Rhada how the husbands felt about their wives becoming literate, and she answered, 'The husbands were initially resistant, but now that the women can read a little, they see how helpful it is to them and their family. '

I then asked her why she volunteered to teach. 'Because I have been fortunate to receive an education, I want to give back. Our village has a commitment to be literate within the next six months, and I'm taking action to fulfil this dream,' she said.

Rhada is sharing her gift of literacy and passing it on to the other women of her village. The joy it gives her, and those in her simple classroom is both moving and inspiring. We all have gifts;

something we can contribute to help others. It doesn't have to be a grand gesture. Any amount of giving is enough to get started.

Things to think about: MAKING A CONTRIBUTION

- As Rhada demonstrates, giving doesn't have to be financial. She shares her gift of literacy to make a meaningful contribution, which not only helps her students, but the whole community. What can you contribute in your workplace or life? What is your special gift?

- I believe everyone has a gift they can share with others. Finding it and expressing it is your contribution to the world. Your special gift might be realised when you're young or old, but as soon as you work out what it is, recognise that it's something you've been given for a reason. So why not use it to help others? Give a lot or give a little – just give something.

KEVIN – THE ANIMATOR

Most of the stories I've shared in this book have been about women. This hasn't been by design. It's more an outcome of an approach that recognises the need for women to be empowered so they can take their rightful place as full and active citizens in their community.

Men also play a significant part in taking action to free their families and community from hunger and poverty. I spent time with one such Ugandan man called Kevin, who lived about two hours from Kampala. Kevin's whole manner warmed my heart.

Kevin was a tall, extremely thin man. His body language was proud and respectful. Kevin was very happy to meet me, and so he dressed in his Sunday best – a brown suit, shirt and tie. His house was a simple two-room dwelling, and he proudly pointed out to me the recently acquired tin roof. He had been a widower for about five years, and was solely responsible for raising and caring for his family of nine children. Kevin is a Hunger Project *animator* (trained volunteer leader) for his village. His commitment to make a difference through ending hunger was luminous.

It was a rainy day when I met Kevin, and his garden looked particularly lush. He farmed about an acre, and had turned land that once had some bananas growing on it and not much else into an agricultural paradise. Kevin pointed out to me all the different vegetables he was growing, as well as his pig, which he had bought using a microfinance loan.

I met some of Kevin's children. It was a Saturday, and a girl of about thirteen was preparing vegetables for the evening meal. Another was caring for some younger children. The elder children were now in school instead of remaining at home.

Beyond his home and family, what was remarkable about Kevin was his broader vision for his community. You see, Kevin also mentors ten other men in his village to follow his example. Even though he is extremely busy looking after his own children, trying to grow enough food to feed them as well as enough to sell at the market, Kevin still manages to find enough time to work as an *animator* and empower others. One of the commitments you make to become an *animator* is not just to look after your own interests, but to be a leader for others. Kevin took this pledge to heart.

Despite Kevin's busy schedule, he rides his borrowed Epicentre bike many miles each week and spends time helping others. He clearly has a lot to do in his own life with his nine children and garden to tend. He also has an ambitious vision for achieving more with his land, by expanding his crops and planting different varieties of vegetables that people at the markets could purchase. He was also trying to figure out a way to transport his produce. I asked him why he had taken this extra responsibility to train others upon himself. His response was twofold.

Firstly, Kevin lives in a community and he feels compelled to help: 'I've lived with these families side-by-side for years. I don't want to be the only one coping and doing well if I'm surrounded by hunger and poverty,' he said. He wanted to live in a community that was thriving, and he knew he could step up and be part of the plan to make that happen.

His second reason was based on the concept of 'security'. He believed that when others raised their quality of life, he and his family would be more secure and prosperous. He did not want his solo success to make him a target for robbery.

Kevin's answers left me pondering for ages. I was struck both by his authentic self-interest, as well as his sophisticated understanding about what makes a person (or a world) secure. We are more secure when others around us are as well. Who wants to live in an area where you inhabit a mansion, but your streets are dirty and your neighbours have nothing? This is an idea worth spreading. Taking action to help others can be wonderfully self-serving. To have a world that is worth living in, we can't act like we live in a bubble. The more we contribute to the growth of ourselves and others, the more security we all will have.

Kevin waved goodbye to me and set off down the dirt road full of potholes on his bike. He was off to speak to some men about composting.

Things to think about: SECURITY

- Kevin's wisdom reminded me of a Benedictine golden rule I once read which said: 'Abandon the search for security. It is futile.' How much of our fear and, therefore, our energy is devoted to making us more secure? This energy is expended on the externals but overlooks a central truth about security and wealth. Namely, you are only as wealthy (or secure) as you are with no money.

- I'm passionate about strengthening the security that comes from resilience, compassion and community. By helping others in the workplace and at home, we are more likely to build a solid foundation that is prosperous, supportive and, ultimately, satisfying and successful.

CHITRA, SATNI AND JULIE – YOUTH ENDING HUNGER

Youth Ending Hunger (YEH, pronounced 'Yay!') is a nationwide volunteer movement of over one hundred thousand school and university students from across Bangladesh. In a country the size of the Australian state of Tasmania, but with more than one hundred and fifty million people, the power and energy of young people can be a huge resource.

To become members of YEH, young people complete three days of training where they realise that they can be a part of plan for creating a Bangladesh that is self-reliant. They then commit to taking action to make this dream a reality. This is a life-changing revelation for them. Try for a moment to imagine living in a country which has been dependent on foreign aid for years, with many children suffering from severe malnutrition, and then realising that something can be done about it. Who wants to be on that team? Yes, please! It really fires up the imagination!

YEH runs campaigns of activities. Sometimes they distribute Oral Rehydration Therapy, a mixture of salt and sugar, which when taken with water can save a child's life from diarrhoeal dehydration. They may also participate in actions to remove plastic bags from Dhaka (Bangladesh's congested capital city), which can precipitate urban flooding during monsoons when drains are clogged.

Education is an understandable focus for YEH members. On a visit to Bangladesh, I went to a school in the south-west of the country. This school was in a small village where I knew opportunities were few. However, there I saw a group of young primary students learning under a tin roof. They were remedial students who had fallen behind in their studies and faced a real danger of dropping out of school. Teaching in this makeshift classroom were three wonderful high school students: Chitra, Satni and Julie.

These girls lived in the village and attended high school. Their schooling levels ranged from Year Nine through to Year Twelve. They were remarkable. Every morning and afternoon after school, they devoted time to teaching the younger remedial students. They didn't get paid to do this. They didn't get extra credit from their high school, either. Yet, every day, Chitra, Satni and Julie taught their young students.

I asked the girls why they spent every day (and all of their spare time) teaching these children. Their unhesitating response was visionary: 'We are committed to having no illiteracy in our village, and this is our contribution to making that happen'.

Things to think about: GETTING INVOLVED

- Don't judge who should be the people 'giving back'. Anyone can do it. Not just those in power, or with lots of money. Young people, old people – anyone can do it!

- Leading with your vision, and helping others actually creates a world that is better for you too. These three young women demonstrate this principle.

- By getting involved, we are having a say in the direction of our world. By sitting on the sidelines and not getting involved, things will stay as they are. Take action, expend your energy – be it financial, time, expertise – in a direction where your hopes and dreams lie. This is the only way we can ever really make any significant change.

Epilogue

One of the reasons I'm so passionate about this idea of ordinary people being *Unlikely Leaders* is because I too am one. I've lived these Nine Steps of Transformative Leadership myself. I started this book with a description of my eye-opening visit to Ethiopia many years ago, and this epilogue is the story of how I got there. It is the story of an *Unlikely Leader*.

I grew up in Perth, Western Australia – the most isolated city in the world – as the second of seven children. I was an average student in high school, and studied politics and English at university – mostly to put off making any decision about the rest of my life. My grades were pretty average. I was unfocused and easily distracted. My big passion in life was music. I loved punk and indie rock and roll, which was an all-consuming extracurricular activity for me. I wasn't the person who was on the student council or involved in special clubs. I was the girl coming in late to classes after a big night of music and fun!

After completing my university degree, I worked with friends who toured bands to Perth, and I helped run a nightclub, so we had a place to party that played the music we liked. Lots of fun times!

My point is that I was definitely not a person fast-tracked for social change. There was no halo above my head. I wasn't a concerned and activist student. I certainly wasn't someone who earnestly beavered away trying to make a difference in the world. Far from it in fact!

Home again after university and travel, I was in Perth when a friend invited me to attend a town hall-type meeting on peace and nuclear disarmament. This was way outside my comfort zone, but, like Flora in Chapter 1, I turned up. It was incredible! I was exposed to concepts and ideas I'd never considered, and I found myself drawn to this issue and to global awareness activism. This was my first contact with making a difference, and it surprised me. *Me? How could I make a difference?* I thought.

I started out running the volunteer and mobilising arm of a tightly fought (and ultimately victorious) national election campaign for an independent senator. I was asked to be involved and, even though I thought I wasn't capable, I said, 'Yes', because it was work that needed to be done. I followed this up by working for that senator in federal politics. I was part of a small team that created the constitution and beginnings of the Greens Party in Western Australia.

It was during this time that I first heard of The Hunger Project. My boss, the senator, talked to us about it. I confess I was not persuaded. *A billion mouths to feed*, was my first thought. It seemed impossible to make any impact on world hunger. I felt overwhelmed just thinking about it, so I did nothing.

I met and fell in love with my husband and had my first child. I left politics and was involved in working on different projects. Life was good. In many ways, I had hit a sweet spot. I had a pleasant life. I had work I liked and was married to a man I loved. However, I just felt like something was missing. I started to question the purpose of life. *What are we here for?* I would think to myself. *Is this it? Am I just going to keep doing more of this, then I'll die and that's it?*

I would catch myself and think, *Get a grip, Cathy!* I'd psychologise: *What's your problem? You are living a life of luxury. You have a fantastic life.* All of this was true; however, berating myself wasn't helpful. I couldn't quell a feeling of dissatisfaction and low-level unhappiness, but I felt I couldn't share it with others as it seemed indulgent. (At the time I thought I was weird, but I now know many people experience similar feelings.)

This discomfort triggered a great period of personal growth. I reflected, I attended personal development workshops, I learned to meditate and I read some fantastic books to get some perspective. I was introduced to philosophers and thinkers like Joseph Campbell, Krishnamurti and others. This opened a whole new world for me. I started to see that this feeling was not unique and nothing new. It had been identified and explored by other people through the ages.

I came across a great line attributed to Martha Graham, the iconic choreographer. She called it 'divine dissatisfaction'. When I read about 'divine dissatisfaction' it nailed it for me. I started to understand that this feeling was natural, and it was linked to our evolution as human beings. It is intrinsic to our growth and development; it is the discomfort that urges us out into the world to be who we can be and to not just settle for what we've got. It's a natural part of being human. Like a bird is meant to fly, humans are meant to stretch, grow and evolve. This cannot happen in our comfort-zone bubble.

I came into contact again with The Hunger Project. This time though, I felt receptive to its mission. I'd just had my first child, and as I held my baby in my arms, I thought, *There's absolutely no way that any parent cannot love their kids and want them to survive and thrive.*

I began to research The Hunger Project and felt excited about what it stood for and what its aims were. I got involved in a small way.

Then one day something confronting, startling and life changing happened. My husband, Steve, and I were asked to consider giving a substantial amount of money to The Hunger Project and become what is called a *Global Investor.* My reaction was less than charitable! I thought: *Are you crazy? There's no way we can do this. We're not rich. In fact, we're far from it.* It triggered my financial survival button!

Now, Steve and I were not what you would consider to be a financially wealthy couple. At this time, he was working in his own small business as a landscape architect, and I was working part-time and caring for our child. This was a lot of money, and we didn't have it lying around in our bank account.

When we were asked to give that money, I started to think of all the other things I could do with it that would be more 'responsible'. We could put it into our mortgage: that would make sense. Or upgrade our car. Or go on a holiday. We could extend our home. I thought about our kids and their education. Shouldn't we be putting this money towards school fees? There seemed to be so many more 'sensible' things to do with it! (It's funny now when I look back on all the cultural conditioning I had then about how to spend money – my scarcity mindset and what I thought would make me happy and secure.)

Becoming a *Global Investor*, and giving such a large amount of money to help end hunger and poverty seemed like an extremely impractical thing for us to do. But it really called to me. I realised that I had enough stuff. Sure, I could have more, but really, what felt more important to me was being a part of something that was more than just my own life and my own comforts.

For us, it came down to having a say in shaping the world we wanted to be involved in, and not leaving it to faceless others and hoping for the best. This is my world and how money is used in our world really matters. I didn't just want to be a consumer. I felt that this act of financial leadership would feed me in a way that I desired to be fed. Steve felt the same way.

So we gave the money, or 'invested' it, as we say in The Hunger Project. This act caused an incredible and surprising expansiveness. I learned something about my relationship to money. I began to understand money was more than just an inert substance. I had an experience of money as a flow of energy. Additionally, through becoming part of The Hunger Project's Global Investment Group, I was also connected to others who felt the same way as me.

Giving this money pierced through the scarcity mindset that makes us believe we've only got a small amount, and when we use it, we've got less. But this isn't true. When you give you grow. Money, ideas and your sense of self all grow.

Giving money was an acknowledgement and recognition of the gifts we had, the abundance of our lives, and that there was a bigger game to play. It owned up to the lottery of life and our good fortune to be born where we were. It was also giving action to our intention to make a difference; to actually support the movement around the world of people combining forces to end their hunger. I think the size of the amount of money we gave mattered also. This wasn't simply a token gesture. This was an act of commitment. It was a stretch. It was an amount that we would notice and feel. It was an amount that gave us life!

We had to structure our work differently to be able to afford the investment, but the biggest change we made was to become much more conscious of how we spent our money. It's amazing how much money we fritter away unconsciously: coffee, muffins, eating out because we can't be bothered cooking. Random spontaneous purchasing. Cha-ching, cha-ching, cha-ching! We became much clearer where our money went. As many a wise person has said: 'I'll tell you what you're committed to by looking at your bank statement!'

Each time Steve and I wrote a cheque to The Hunger Project, it was an incredible feeling. It felt like a punch in the air. It was a clear statement of who we were and what we were committed to. This was not an ego thing – we didn't even particularly tell people about it. It was just that something clicked into place.

(Heeding this call to invest started something profound for us, and over the years, we've continued investing in The Hunger Project. We've also got our kids involved in the discussion, which has built a rich family awareness about money and what we can do with it.)

Around this time we accepted an invitation to go on a leadership trip to Ethiopia with The Hunger Project – paying our own way, of course! And, as you've already read in the beginning of this book, this trip completely changed the direction of my life.

I came back to Perth a different person. I'd been in the villages where hunger and poverty were endemic. I *knew*. After what I'd seen, I couldn't pretend that I didn't know.

I was still working and raising my small family, so I wasn't about to race off to become an aid worker, or renounce the world and become a nun. I searched my heart for what I could do – a young woman from a small remote city – to keep my promise to the people in Goda Chili. You'll understand now from the stories in this book that the solution is not for all of us to go over to Africa and dig wells. So what part could I play in the movement to end world hunger?

It became clear to me that I needed to help raise the money to ensure the people most affected by hunger became the ones most empowered and qualified to end it. It is critical that money flows into work that builds *Unlikely Leaders*. At the time, I would have loved my part to have been something else! I knew I had to ask people for money, and I dearly wished something else was needed of me. I thought: *I can't ask people for money. I'm not a fundraiser.* When I 'got over myself', I realised that I could.

I leaned into what was needed and asked people to give money to The Hunger Project. People were generous; I think particularly when they sensed that I came from an authentic place. I started small – I vividly remember raising my first $100 – and I have grown from there. I've come to love this aspect of my work. When I ask someone to invest in The Hunger Project, I feel I am channelling two things: the energies and desires of people living in hunger who want to create a better life for themselves, and the desires of people in more developed countries who yearn to contribute, connect and make a difference. I've discovered that many other forms of hunger prevail in the developed world which are linked to our relationship to money and purpose.

When I ask people to give, I'm facilitating an opportunity for them to become more fulfilled and connected. I'm offering a way for them to increase alignment to the deepest yearnings of their being. I've discovered that I'm not trying to *get* something off someone. I'm actually giving them something.

In asking others to give and get involved, the currency might be money, but the invitation is to play a part in shaping a new world for everyone; to take the necessary action so that every person can feed themselves and their families. It is thrilling to still be a *Global Investor*, and see the community grow.

After many years of being a volunteer leader and fundraiser, this *Unlikely Leader* was invited to become a staff member of The Hunger Project. I am still on staff today, passionately serving in the quest to call forth a new world where hunger and poverty are not a daily inevitable humiliation and heartbreak. A world where all of us – regardless of where we live – can offer our love and leadership abilities to change the world.

Next Step

These Nine Steps to Transformative Leadership: Belief in People, Facing Reality, Vision, Personal Responsibility, Collective Power, Creating a Supportive Environment, Finding New Ways, Experiencing Success and Giving Back all highlight a pathway that heralds the way forward for both personal and social change. Throughout this book, we have learnt from women and men across South Asia and Africa. Now it is time for you to put these lessons into practice.

Having read the book this far, you've seen many examples of how, as human beings, we needn't be defined by our circumstances. Understanding this principle is liberating. With this realisation, questions arise: If I am more than my past and my conditioning, then who am I? What am I capable of?

Transforming this insight into action is the next step. What actions can you now take? How differently do you perceive yourself and your world? These Nine Steps reveal how others have done it; however, demonstrating the necessary courage and vision in your own life is up to you. I encourage you to work through the Nine Steps outlined in this book and apply each leadership distinction to the life you want and the world you want.

When it comes to leadership and creating change in our family, our community, our work and our world, we're the ones we've been waiting for! And yes, I'm talking about you!

Through meeting these courageous leaders in this book, it's my wish that you too will be inspired to live a bigger life. I hope you will act on your own potential as an *Unlikely Leader*.

Help Build the Unlikely Leader Movement

In addition to gaining insights through reading this book, every copy sold will have at least 50 per cent of the profit go directly to The Hunger Project to unleash more *Unlikely Leaders*.

If this book has inspired or encouraged you, and you would like to connect more people in the world with the beautiful concept of 'Unlikely Leadership', please share this work in the following ways:

- Find me on Twitter @cathypburke and #unlikelyleaders. You can also also tune into @hungerproject
- Visit www.cathyburke.com for more inspiration.
- Email me at cathy@cathyburke.com with your thoughts, testimonials and video examples of 'Unlikely Leadership' that are turning you on.
- Unleash your money and invest in The Hunger Project's movement to end hunger at www.thp.org.au
- Head over to Cathy Burke and Unlikely Leaders on Facebook. Start a conversation. Post your quotes, thoughts and revelations.
- I lurk on Instagram too.
- Review this book on online book sites. Choose it for your book club. Buy it for your school or work.
- Attend a Rethinking What's Possible workshop. You'll find details for Australia on THP website (www.thp.org.au).

- Keep living your unique ability to make a difference. Be a loving, bold presence in the world. Support yourself, your family and your community to envision and grow towards a better future. Together we can do it!

Thank you

Gratitude

Thank you to all the women and men in villages around the world who have shared your lives with me. Your leadership and courage sets the bar very high for what it means to be human. You are invisible to many, but not to me. I hope I can do justice to your vision by bringing some of your heroic journeys to light. Thank you for the barbequed goat, the chai, the shared times spent under a shady tree, the invitation to sit and talk in a small room in a Dhaka slum. You have taught me so much about resilience, leadership, power and love. I will forever remain your committed partner in ending world hunger.

Thank you to my beautiful husband Steve, and children Bronwen and Patrick. Over the past twenty years, I've been away from home a lot. I've missed family occasions. There are things that I just wasn't able to be there for. You've never complained, and more than this, your love and support for me has given me wings. We're on this journey together. We're a family that stands for something great and this is underpinned with love and respect. I love you all so much. Thank you also Steve and Bronnie for your endless reading, advice and encouragement for the many different drafts of this book. You made it richer and you kept me holding the faith. You were frank, fearless and loving in your insights and recommendations. What a team!

Thank you to The Hunger Project and the millions worldwide who are committed to this glorious endeavour to end global hunger through empowering the hungry themselves. The principles behind this work, and the incredible people involved give huge purpose to my life. There are too many to thank personally, but I do want to pay tribute to these fearless leaders: Badiul, Rita, Dicko, Joan, Åsa, John, Ruchi, Rinky, Rowlands, Madeline, Pascal, Evariste, Daisy, Samuel, Lorena, Neguest, Tarcila and Clara. I'm proud to be by your side. Thank you also to my team (both boards and staff) at THP-A. I love you all and I'm grateful for you *Every.Single.Day.* Thank you for the tea, the laughs and the unyielding commitment.

Thank you to Daniel Priestley, Glen Carlson, Andrew Griffiths and the gang at KPI. I would never have written this book in a million years without you. And to my editors: Stacey Dobis, Annie Reid and Kirsty Ogden, whose thoughtful guidance and rigorous overview have made this a much better book.

Thank you to my six brothers and sisters: Jenny, Donna, Francis, Matt, Andy and Ali. I love our tribal closeness, and our constant support and uplifting attitude toward each other. You guys (and your kids – and cats) are the best sibs anyone could have! To Mum and Dad: your resilience and hope always inspires me.

And thank you dear reader. It is my belief that books find the right person at the right time. I hope the time you spend in these pages illuminates something wonderful for you in your own life about your 'Unlikely Leadership'.

About The Hunger Project

The Hunger Project is a global organisation made up of millions of people. We are deeply committed to ending world hunger, and we're working with others to achieve this goal by 2030.

We have trained more than four hundred thousand local volunteer leaders and we have about three hundred staff all around the world. Our global office is in New York and we operate in twenty-three countries. In 2014, The Hunger Project had a positive impact on nineteen million people in fifteen thousand villages across Africa, South Asia and Latin America.

The movement is spreading, yet there is still a lot more to do. Come and be part of ending world hunger with us.

For more information about The Hunger Project, including how to get involved, please visit: www.thp.org.au

About Cathy Burke

Cathy Burke has something unique and powerful to say about leadership and human potential.

As the CEO for The Hunger Project Australia, Cathy rarely stays long in one place. She is equally at home drinking tea with women in their huts in India, as she is walking through small villages with farmers in Africa, or addressing hundreds of business leaders about personal and cultural change. She is driven by her passionate belief that people are capable of achieving anything – often against the greatest of odds.

Cathy has received numerous accolades for her work on leadership, including winning the prestigious 2014 Westpac and Australian Financial Review 100 Women of Influence Award.

Cathy is a sought-after speaker. Her insights, humour and deep compassion connect and resonate with people and organisations globally.

When she is at home at Byron Bay, she loves eating mangoes, having fun with her family, listening to dirty rock and roll music and dancing in her lounge room.

You can find Cathy online at www.cathyburke.com

Connect with Cathy on Twitter at cathypburke